HARRY LEON WILSON

H. L. W. as sketched by James Montgomery Flagg

Harry Leon Wilson

*Some account of the triumphs and tribulations
of an American popular writer*

by

GEORGE KUMMER

*Associate Professor of English
at Western Reserve University*

THE PRESS OF WESTERN RESERVE UNIVERSITY
CLEVELAND 6, OHIO, U.S.A. • 1963

for

Marguerite

Contents

Preface

I FIRST BECAME ACQUAINTED with the work of Harry Leon Wilson in the nineteen twenties when I read *Professor How Could You!* The delightful characters who capered through that hilarious picaresque romance led me on to *Merton of the Movies, Ruggles of Red Gap* and the robust charms of Ma Pettengill. My study of the Wilson canon was then interrupted, and I did not think of his stories again until years later, when in working up a course in American humor at Western Reserve University, I realized that at least some of them should be included. On consulting the standard bibliographies I found to my surprise almost no material about either the stories or the author. Inquiry among skilled students of the period revealed the lamentable fact that only twenty years after his death the creator of Ma Pettengill, Bunker Bean, and Professor Copplestone was almost forgotten, the victim, as Carl Van Doren noted, of "short-sighted, low-spirited criticism."[1]

I set out to learn what I could about Wilson, and as I accumulated information about his life and writings, both seemed to me to take on significance. His life is an interesting example of a common American pattern: A poor boy through a combination of talent, hard work, and luck achieves considerable success in an exacting calling and then loses everything. Typical, also, of this traditional pattern is the stoutheartedness with which Harry confronted his troubles. He was a past master at the art of keeping a stiff upper lip. "*Nothing ever* got a squeak—not even the briefest or faintest —of self-commiseration out of him," wrote Booth Tarkington, the man who knew him best.[2] As an author, he succeeded in adding several entertaining specimens to the gallery of American humorous types. Admittedly, humor is a perishable commodity, but after a generation a good many of his pages are still funny. As a whole, his work throws a good deal of light upon certain of the attitudes of the middle-class American of his time.

Between Wilson and his public there was an exceptionally warm rapport. In the course of my study many of the older generation have told me that just to hear Harry Leon Wilson's name again makes them smile in happy recollection. I hope they will enjoy this renewal of acquaintance and that younger readers may be led to look up and read the best of Wilson— say *Ruggles of Red Gap* and *Professor How Could You!*

I have not tried to write a blow-by-blow biography. My aim has been to survey Wilson's literary career and accomplishments and to assess the forces which influenced them. Even this I could not have attempted without the cooperation of Wilson's son and daughter, Mr. Leon Wilson and Mrs. Noel Harris, who made available to me their father's correspondence and other family papers. They set no limitations on my use of this material, and so I am wholly responsible for sins of omission and commission.

Permission to quote from unpublished letters has been granted by Miss Alice B. Beer, Chancellor Clifford Cook Furnas, Professor William White Howells, Mr. August Mencken, Mr. James Stevens, Mrs. Julian Street, Mrs. Zilpha Riley, and Mrs. Susanah Tarkington.

For reminiscences or help in research I am indebted to Professor Frederick W. Adrian, Miss Irene Alexander, Mrs. Cleveland Amory, the late Roy Atwell, Mrs. Luellen T. Bussenius, Mr. Witter Bynner, Mrs. Henry Seidel Canby, Professor Oscar Cargill, Mr. Alexander Clark, Mrs. Helen Worden Cranmer, Mr. Homer Croy, Mrs. H. H. Fisher, Chancellor C. C. Furnas of the University of Buffalo, Mrs. Ernest Dewald, Mr. Hugh McNair Kahler, the late Fred C. Kelly, Mrs. Grace Hegger Lewis, Mr. Albert Lawson, Professor Ralph McCanse, the late Adelaide Neall, Miss Lee O'Neill, Mr. Paul O'Neill, Mr. Henry L. Perry, Mrs. Katherine Pinkerton, the late Kenneth Roberts, Mr. Willis Thornton, and Professor Franklin Walker.

I have also received various favors from the Manuscripts Division of the Bancroft Library of the University of California at Berkeley, the California State Library, the Carmel Public Library, the Cleveland Public Library, the Library of the Historical Society of Pennsylvania, the Henry E. Huntington Library and Art Gallery, the Illinois State Historical Library, the Kansas State Historical Society, the New York Public Library, the Princeton University Library, the National Archives and Records Service, Street and Smith, the *Saturday Evening Post,* and the Union Pacific Railroad. Western Reserve University granted me a semester's leave to work on the book.

Finally, I want to thank my friends, Professor Carl Wittke, Professor William Powell Jones and Professor Lyon Richardson, for their perceptive interest.

GEORGE KUMMER

Cleveland, Ohio
September 1963

Notes on the Preface

1. *The American Novel,* Revised and enlarged edition (New York: The Macmillan Company, 1940), p. 270.

2. Unpublished letter to Miss Adelaide Neall, who was for many years secretary to George Horace Lorimer, June 30, 1939.

Little Arcady

To MANY AMERICANS the news of Harry Leon Wilson's death in June, 1939 brought a sense of personal loss. Ever since his stories began appearing in the *Saturday Evening Post* in 1912, thousands of people all over the country had read him with delight, and many of them had come to regard characters like Bunker Bean, Ma Pettengill, Ruggles, Cousin Egbert, Professor Copplestone, Merton Gill, and the flapper with her "little old last year's car" almost as members of their own households. Hundreds of readers had written letters to the magazine in Independence Square commending Wilson as a benefactor. To Thomas Beer his name brought up a recollection of how his own father, now dead these many years, used to enjoy Wilson's *Puck*.[1] An obituary editorial in *The New York Herald Tribune*[2] voiced the feeling that Wilson had indeed been one of ours. "Others," said the newspaper, "have attempted loftier flights. But in the air that Wilson breathed he was a master, and the result was not so much a record of the country, its scene, its salient folk, their bedevilment and their victory as the essence of the soil itself. Harry Leon Wilson was America."

1

There are many Americas. The one to which the obituary editorial referred was certainly not the America of 1939, a country just emerging from the hard times of the thirties and about to plunge into the Second World War. Harry Leon Wilson's America was the West and Middle West of the eighteen-eighties and nineties, a rude, bucolic land whose history, as Harry said, spanned scarcely more than two generations: "We are so ancient that plenty of us remember the stone fireplace in the log-cabin, with its dusters for the hearth of buffalo tail and wild-turkey wing, with iron pot hung from the chimney hook, with pewter or wooden plates from which to eat with horn-handled spoons. But we are so modern that we have fine new houses with bay windows, ornamental cupolas, and porches raving woodenly in that frettish fever which the infamous scroll-saw put upon fifty years of our land's domestic architecture. And these houses are furnished with splendid modern furniture, even with black walnut, gold touched and upholstered in blue plush and maroon, fresh from the best factories. Our fairly old people remember when they hunted deer and were hunted by the Red Indian on our town site, while their grandchildren have only the memories of the townborn, of the cottage-organ, the novel railroad, and the two-story brick block with ornamental false front. In short, we round an epoch within ourselves, historically and socially."[3]

This description, when Harry wrote it in 1905, could have applied to almost any small town in the upper Mississippi valley, but the one he had in mind was Oregon, Illinois, the county seat of Ogle County, where he passed the first sixteen years of his life. For him this was a crucial period, for almost everything in his later career had its roots in his family background and his boyhood environment.

Harry's father, Samuel Wilson, and his mother Adeline, née Kidder, and their four children—Florence, aged twelve; May, eight; Lester, six; and Samuel, three—settled in Oregon in

1862. Both Samuel and Adeline were natives of Chautauqua County, New York, where Samuel had edited the *Fredonia Advertiser*. From there they migrated to Council Bluffs, Iowa in 1858 and then to a farm near Winnebago, Illinois before finally moving to Oregon.[4] There Samuel, who followed the printer's trade, was able to establish his own newspaper, *The Oregon National Guard*, in June, 1866.

An able and energetic editor, Samuel succeeded in making the *Guard* one of the liveliest weeklies in northern Illlinois, but in spite of its distinction, it never became a prosperous business. The reason was Samuel's politics; he was, as Harry later said, "a natural born Democrat."[5] In northern Illinois, the country of Grant and Lincoln, in the years following the Civil War, Democratic papers were bound to suffer. Certainly Samuel could not hope for any subsidy in the shape of county printing, the bread and butter of most small-town papers in that era. In a Republican stronghold like Ogle County—which even in 1932 gave Herbert Hoover 8,224 votes to Franklin D. Roosevelt's 5,416—*The Guard* was doomed from the start.

Ironically, the views that penalized Samuel Wilson then are precisely those endorsed by conservative Republicans now. "The intention of *The Guard*," said the editor on June 6, 1866 in his first issue, "is to endorse the great and vital principles of Democracy—that government is rather a necessity than a desideratum, and being a necessity should be limited as much as possible, and allowed to abridge no more of the natural rights of individuals than is absolutely necessary—that laws and constitutions should be allowed no loose construction, and no elements of extension, but should be confined to their plainly invested powers, under a strictly literal construction." Stubborn as a donkey, Samuel clung to this creed come hell or high water. He had served in the Union army and admired Ulysses S. Grant as a military leader, but in the campaign of 1868 he did not hesitate to tell his readers that Grant's initials stood for "Usually Stewed" or that the General was "the bondholder's candidate."[6] Even the decisive Republican victory in that election failed to silence Wilson. "Democratic principles," he told his readers, "now unpopular through false teaching will sooner or later prevail . . . the editor is poor but he's going on with the Guard."[7]

Samuel's defiance was not quite so heroic as it sounds. Being poor in Oregon in 1868 was not an insupportable fate. The Wilsons were never in actual want, and in some ways Samuel was lucky. He never had to worry about payments on the car, the electric refrigerator, the washing machine, or the television set, never had to fear that the gas, electricity, or telephone would be cut off, for these marvels had not yet reached Oregon. He lighted his house with kerosene lamps, and his boys easily gathered the wood which his wife burned in the kitchen range. But money was scarce; some things like coal for the stove in the front room and newsprint and taxes had to be paid for in cash. Much of the time Samuel felt hard put to it.

Harassed as he was by poverty and ill health—for he was already suffering from the tuberculosis which eventually killed him—Samuel may well have regarded with mixed feelings the birth of his fifth child—Harry Leon—which occurred on May 1, 1867. At any rate it was the *Reporter*, the *Guard's* Republican rival, which first noted that a "young editor" of the *Guard* had arrived in town, and quoted Samuel as saying he "is one of the heavy guns that will always be heard." To this the *Guard* replied that he was certainly "a pound and three quarters heavier than the late lithographed edition of the *Reporter*."[8]

According to his sister May, who always had an especial fondness for him, Harry was a fine, healthy baby who gave the family little trouble. Like the other Wilson children, as soon as he was old enough to be of any use, he was put to work in the printing office, and the dirt and litter of the place were among his early memories. From the first he regarded his father, a lean, muscular man, who stood five feet nine inches tall and had piercing black eyes, black hair, and a long black beard, as a stern and exacting taskmaster, grimly and senselessly opposed to anything pleasant like chewing tobacco or smoking. One day someone gave the lad several leaves of tobacco which he brought into the shop.

"What's that for?" demanded Samuel.

"To smoke," replied Harry.

"Well, let's see it smoke," snapped Samuel, and, confiscating the tobacco, he tossed it into the stove.[9]

"He was always my enemy. Even when he wasn't riding me, I felt his disapproval," the novelist told his own children fifty years later. Occasions for disapproval were numerous, for Harry, boylike, preferred pleasures like fishing and baseball to constructive activities like splitting kindling, weeding the garden, setting type, folding papers, sweeping out, and once a week inking the Washington hand press while his father ran off the edition. This last, a dirty, disagreeable chore, consisted of distributing the ink over the two forms of type on the press bed by means of a roller. His father across the press would then let down a frame in which he had fixed a virgin sheet of paper, run the bed of the press back under a weighted shelf, and pull a mighty lever to make the imprint. For a long time the boy thought the pulling of the lever was what his father meant by the phrase "the power of the press."

The only task in the office he really liked was operating the job press, the energy for which he furnished by moving his foot up and down on a treadle. When the press opened its maw, he would pull out the printed card or bill and put in another before the jaws closed down. It was thrilling, because he knew that if he kept his hand in there until the jaws came together he might not have it any longer.

Failure to perform his duties was apt to result in the

bearded tyrant's conducting the boy to the woodshed for a switching. Harry resented these punishments so much that even in adult life he never really forgave his father. As a boy in his daydreams he often turned upon the tyrant, gave him a severe drubbing, and then escaped to the West. What kept him from trying to make this dream come true was, he said, "fear."[10]

To other people Samuel did not seem to be the ogre Harry thought him. When he died, a fellow editor characterized him as "a kind friend, a wit, and a philosopher," and his daughter May, twelve years older than Harry, regarded him with deep affection and considered it no hardship to help out by setting type for the *Guard*. In her later years she liked to recall how much "Pa" enjoyed gathering the family about him for an evening of song. All of the Wilsons had good voices and in the summer when these concerts occurred on the front porch the neighbors along the street would gather to enjoy and vigorously applaud such numbers as "Those Evening Bells,"

> Those evening bells, those evening bells,
> How many a tale their music tells,
> Of youth and home and that sweet time
> When last I heard their soothing chime,
> When last I heard their soothing chime.[11]

Moreover, he seems to have been a sociable person, for he belonged to the Masons, and the files of the *Guard*[12] indicate that in spite of his formidable whiskers and severe manner he had a sense of humor. He frequently printed extracts from Josh Billings and Mark Twain as well as traditional rustic pleasantries like "a transcendentalist is one who has soarings after the infinite and divings after the unfathomable, but who does not like to pay cash," and "the proper retort to Parson Brownlow's assertion that he would vote the radical Republican ticket if the ballot box were placed in the jaws of hell is that every man has a right to vote in his own precinct." Harry

Leon Wilson may well have inherited his sense of humor from the father he so cordially disliked.

Harry always felt much closer to his mother than to his father. A little lady, who, as the novelist recalled, "liked to wear lavender and to sing," she was a descendent of William Brewster, who landed from the Mayflower on Plymouth rock.[13] The romantic, sentimental side of Harry's nature probably came to him through her. Certainly she humored his boyish fancies. One day when he was five or six he decided to set out on a long journey. His feelings had not been hurt, he was not angry, he simply wanted to see the world; and so bidding goodbye to his mother and his niece Mabel, incidentally only two years younger than her Uncle Harry and his constant playmate, he started out. Actually, he merely went across an adjoining cornfield and a fence, but when he was called for lunch, he insisted he was on the other side of the ocean and couldn't come. Since Mabel refused to eat if Harry had no food, his mother had her place sandwiches on a stump where he could get them. When darkness finally forced the young Odysseus in, he pretended he had been gone for years. "I see," he remarked to his mother, "you've still got the same old cat."[14]

In Fredonia the Wilsons had been Episcopalians. In Oregon there weren't enough adherents of that denomination to maintain a church, although in the late seventies and early eighties a curate would occasionally visit the village and summon the faithful to worship in the county courthouse. Harry recalled being baptized there and how on emerging from the service "feeling vastly superior and freshly made over," he condescended to salute his lowly Methodist chum from the lofty courthouse steps.[15]

Probably because Harry's maternal grandfather, Silas Kidder, had been a ruling elder in the Presbyterian church in Westfield, New York,[16] whenever there were no Episcopalian services the Wilsons worshipped with the Presbyterians. On those Sundays Harry was thoroughly miserable. Throughout his boyhood the doctrine of infant damnation worried him greatly, and as an adult he took his revenge by assailing it vigorously in the pages of *Puck*[17] and also in his novel *The Seeker*,[81] where he gives what purports to be an essay on "Elisha and the Wicked Children" written by a pious lad of ten:

> "This lesson," the composition began, "is to teach us to love God and the prophets or else we will all likely get into trouble. It says Elisha went up from Bethel and some children came out of the city and said go up thou Baldhead. They said it twice one after the other and so Elisha got mad right away and turned around and cursed them good in the name of the Lord and so 2 She Bears come along and et up 42 of them for Elisha was a holy prophet of God and had not ought to of been yelled at. So of course the mothers would take on very much when they found their 42 Children et up but I think that we had ought to learn from this that these 42 little ones was not the Elected. It says in our cathchism God having out of his mere good pleasure elected some to everlasting life. Now God being a Presbiterian would know these 42 little ones had not been elected so they might as well be et up by bears as anything else to show forth his honour and glory Forever Amen. It should teach a Boy to be mighty carful about kidding old men unless he is a Presbiterian. I spelled every word in this right."

If religion as professed in Oregon in Harry's boyhood impressed him unfavorably, education as offered in the local school had a similar effect: in 1930 he said in a newspaper interview that he still could not pass a school building "without shudders of repulsion."[19] His dislike of formal education is reflected in one of the most amusing passages in *The Boss of Little Arcady*[20] in which he pokes fun at the absurdities of the school readers. The selection was entitled "A Good Investment" and began

"Will you lend me two thousand dollars to establish myself in a small retail business?" inquired a young man not yet out of his teens of a middle-aged gentleman who was poring over his ledger in the counting room of one of the largest establishments in Boston.

For a moment the middle-aged gentleman regarded the young man with a look of surprise. Then he inquired, "What security can you give me?" To which the latter answered, "Nothing but my note."

"Which I fear would be below par in the market," replied the merchant, smiling.

"Perhaps so," said the young man, "but Mr. Barton, remember that the boy is not the man; the time may come when Hiram Strosser's note will be as readily accepted as that of any other man."

The lesson then told how the kindly Mr. Barton finally loaned Hiram Strosser the money, after vainly asking Mr. Hawley, a wealthy merchant of Milk Street, "to share half the risk." Ten years later, when Mr. Barton because of the failure of his London bankers, faced disaster, Hiram was able to lend him $75,000, the amount needed to tide him over the crisis. But Mr. Hawley, who was also embarrassed by the failure of the London bankers, had no trustful friend to tide him over and the outcome was bankruptcy. The story ended with a stroke of poetical justice. Mr. Barton had the satisfaction of telling Mr. Hawley about Hiram's check and of reminding him that he too had once had the opportunity to become "a co-benefactor of that upright and open-handed youth;" whereupon the deservedly ruined Hawley "moved on, dejected and sad, while Mr. Barton returned to his establishment cheered and animated."

The lesson typified for Harry the basic weakness of school readers: they gave one false ideas about life, filling minds with romantic fantasies corresponding to nothing in the real world. Much as Harry loved words, he always kept a strong grip on facts.

More important to him than anything he studied in school was the reading he did on his own. He liked Bret Harte and Dickens, but his favorite author was Mark Twain. In June 1936 he told his son Leon, who was then in Hollywood working on a moving picture version of *Tom Sawyer,* that Twain was "my earliest idol:"

> Tom Sawyer furnished me with a violent flutter of ecstasy and I can still see, as in print, the first line, the opening words with which Aunt Polly calls the errant Tom. And I am still strong for my next MT book, Roughing It. I have the idea it would still entertain me though I read it so much and so often. (In the fore part of the volume was a sassy blue paster reading "This volume stolen from the public library of Oregon, Illinois.") Later came the Tramp Abroad and Innocents Abroad, both of which dulled a bit the blade of my hunger. I wondered if I were growing up or if Clemens was. In later years I saw things of his that freed me from any guilt; things pretty noisy and clumsy. But first chance I have I shall nail a copy of Roughing It and see if it doesn't get me again after sixty years or so. I suspect it will. Don't ever get to thinking Clemens wasn't a real one, because he was.[21]

In a later letter Harry added that "if *Tom Sawyer* isn't the first book I really read, it's at least the one I best remember after sixty years." He also recalled that his copy was bound "in blue cloth with gilt lettering."[22] In a still later letter he continued to defend his idol:

I know you don't regard Tom Sawyer highly as a book. I think that is chiefly because your own boyhood was so different from his. With me it was quite the contrary. There was my own life—public and private—my dreams and frustrations, tragedies and comedies—put into plain print—which was nothing short of magic. But that was because I had that same boyhood life.[23]

Like many another boy Harry identified with Tom Sawyer. Though Tom lived in a different section of the country and in a different period, Harry knew exactly how he felt about school and Sunday school. He knew too how Tom felt about the river, for though the Rock, a sizable tributary of the Mississippi, was much too crooked and too full of concealed obstructions for profitable steamboating, it was a wonderful place to swim and fish, and it afforded Harry many chances to make a little spending money by rowing picnickers over to the Island. It was natural that in Harry's own writing Twain should become an important influence.

Harry developed into a sturdy lad, well able to take care of himself in any tussle with boys of his own age. No rowdy ever jeeringly threw Harry's hat on some high roof or spat on his new shoes with impunity. Though not a bully, he was mischievous and sometimes provoked fights. A prankster, he liked to approach a contemporary with some such remark as "They're going to tear down the courthouse," and if the other boy fell for it and asked "What for?" Harry would reply "Cat fur to make kitten britches of." Whereupon a conflict would often ensue.

With his companions he enjoyed roaming over the remarkably beautiful country surrounding Oregon. A favorite spot of his was Eagle's Nest,[24] a high bluff some five miles above the village, which as Reuben Gold Thwaites said afforded a view of "one of the finest river and forest landscapes in the Mississippi basin."[25] Aside from the never-to-be-resolved conflict with his father, Harry's boyhood seems to have been quite normal. It ended with the death of his father on November 5, 1883. Long before that event Samuel had had to give up his newspaper, and by 1882 he was too ill with tuberculosis to work at his trade as a printer. In that crisis, Harry, now fifteen, left school, and went to work in Oregon's leading industry, a furniture factory, where for ten hours of drudgery he was paid fifty cents a day.[26] His mother, hoping a change of climate would be curative, somehow scraped together enough money to send Samuel to Nevada, but the long trip only fatigued the poor man, who after a few lonesome, homesick weeks returned to Oregon, where he died soon afterward.[27]

Though Samuel Wilson was buried from the Presbyterian church, he was not an orthodox believer. During his long illness he speculated much on immortality, without coming to any conclusion. "He has solved that great problem," said one obituary, " a question over which he and the writer have had many long talks. He went fearlessly and hopefully into the unseen and we doubt not has found a welcome there."[28] His father's skeptical attitude may have strengthened the strong anti-religious views Harry held in later life.

A few weeks after his father's death the Wilson family left Oregon, Harry's mother going to live with his married sister in Rockford while Harry went to Topeka, Kansas where his brother, Lester, eleven years older than he, took care of him.[29] Lester, who had a job as secretary to the governor of Kansas, offered to teach Harry typing and shorthand. Harry accepted with alacrity. He never forgot that Lester rescued him from a job he hated, and years later when Lester got into financial difficulties Harry loyally stood by him.

Harry was always proud of his heritage as a small-town Mid-westerner. Provincial to his finger tips, he enjoyed reading fiction like E. W. Howe's *The Story of a Country Town,* Homer Croy's *West of the Water Tower,* and Ruth Suckow's short stories, though he himself never attempted to treat the

small town in realistic detail.[30] His talent was rather for farce
and caricature, and he stuck to it. Within his limits, however, he was diverting. Take for example his account of Mrs.
Aurelia Potts, the grass widow from Boston who on arriving
in Little Arcady is appalled at the intellectual sterility of the
place. Determining to do something about this condition, she
calls the opinion leaders of the village together, reads them a
long paper she has composed on "The Message of Emerson,"
and then sets about to reform the English of the *Daily Argus*.
Hear her at work on the editor's prose:

> "I turn now from mere solecisms to the broader
> question of taste. Under the heading 'Hanged in
> Carroll County,' I read an item beginning, 'At eight-
> thirty A.M. last Friday the soul of Martin G. Buckley,
> dressed in a neat-fitting suit of black, with a low col-
> lar and black cravat, was ushered into the presence
> of his God.' Pardon me, but do we not find here, if
> we read closely, an attempt to blend the material
> with the spiritual with a result that we can only
> designate as infelicitous?"[31]

Next Mrs. Potts decides that the editor as well as his prose
needs reforming, and so she marries him, bears him twin sons
whom she names Hays and Wheeler after the Republican
standard-bearers in the current election, and in addition to
fulfilling all her duties as mother and assistant to the editor
gets herself elected as delegate to the National Federation of
Women's Clubs. Certainly this energetic lady did a good deal
for the town.

Harry might laugh at the people of Little Arcady, but his
laughter is never contemptuous, since unlike Sinclair Lewis,
he identified with them. The author of *Main Street* was his
pet aversion. "Why," Harry asked Tarkington, "can't I read
Sinclair Lewis with any comfort? Is it merely because a few
days' personal encounter left me disliking him? Some years

ago I approached Main Street with lively anticipation (as for any small town stuff). To my surprise I couldn't do it. Decided it must be because I knew so well just what he was going to do. A couple of later ones I found simply boring. Then lately I did read the hotel one (work of art is it?) after which I believe I have the secret of his unpleasant effect on me—it is that on every page he is taking pains to show me his superiority to his people—his contemptuous smarty superiority—and I am tired of the constant reminder."[32]

Harry always defended the small town from the assaults of writers like Lewis. In 1922 when the "revolt from the village" was at its height he made a point which anticipated Bernard DeVoto's *The Literary Fallacy* by twenty-two years. Speaking through the mouth of Ma Pettengill he observed, "the small town—in fact all American towns—is getting hell from a lot of writers. . . . But having been around the map quite some, it is my hunch that the United States has more in it than these nagging writers give it credit for when they set out to be smart . . . a writer can't see a bit more in any town than what he has in himself, so maybe the trouble lies there."[33]

Provincial America did well by Harry Leon Wilson. It watched eagerly for his serials in *The Saturday Evening Post,* it furnished material for his stories, it laughed at his humor, and it rejoiced in his success. The people of his home town followed his career with interest. Nine years after he had left Oregon the *Ogle County News,* whose editor had learned his trade under Samuel Wilson, announced that Harry had accepted a job on *Puck* in New York and predicted that he would win "fame and fortune" there.

Though Harry lived for some time in Paris, though he knew Europe and the world quite as thoroughly as did most of the critics who touted *Main Street,* he always remained a spokesman for small town attitudes. He was willing to agree that the rays of the sun first touched Manhattan's topless towers, but he was convinced that a few beams, here and there, reached the hinterland. The knowledge of the tastes and attitudes of the plain people which he absorbed during his boyhood in Little Arcady were decidedly useful to him when he attempted to point up the incongruities of their lives in his fiction.

Notes on the Text

The following abbreviations have been used in the notes: HLW *for Harry Leon Wilson;* TP *for Tarkington Papers in the Princeton University Library;* WP *for Wilson Papers in the possession of Mr. Leon Wilson; and* HSP *for the Historical Society of Pennsylvania.*

CHAPTER ONE

Little Arcady

1. "Harry Leon Wilson, The Man from Home," *New York Herald Tribune Books,* June 16, 1935, p. 1.

2. June 30, 1939.

3. *The Boss of Little Arcady* (Boston: Lothrop, Lee & Shepard Co., 1905), pp. 35–36.

4. "Adeline Wilson, Wife of Pioneer Ogle Co., Editor, Gone from Life," *Rockford (Ill.) News,* September 16, 1914; Letter, Albert Lawson, Rockford, Illinois, to the author, February 1, 1958. Samuel Wilson was Mr. Lawson's great, great grandfather.

5. Notes taken by Charis Wilson Harris and Leon Wilson of some conversations with HLW begun on May 21, 1938. WP. Hereafter cited as C and L's Notes.

6. *The Guard,* June 24, 1868; July 15, 1868.

7. *Ibid.,* December 2, 1868.

8. *Ibid.,* May 8, 1867.

9. C and L's Notes.

10. "Naughty Boys," *The Saturday Evening Post*, CXCI, (May 3, 1919), pp. 3–4.

11. Letter, May Wilson Miller to HLW, January 22, 1915 enclosing a copy of "Those Evening Bells," in Samuel Wilson's handwriting. WP.

12. November 27, 1867; May 1, 1867.

13. Morgan Stafford, *A Genealogy of the Kidder Family* (Rutland, Vt.: Tuttle Publishing Co., 1941), p. 231.

14. May Wilson Miller told this anecdote to Mrs. Zilpha Riley, who related it to the author in an interview on March 29, 1958.

15. C and L's Notes.

16. Obed Edson, *History of Chautauqua County, New York* (Boston: W. A. Fergusson & Company, 1894), p. 586.

17. "A Light That Failed," *Puck*, February 16, 1893.

18. (New York: Doubleday, Page and Co., 1904), pp. 14–15.

19. Marion L. Starkey, "Harry Leon Wilson in California," *Boston Transcript, Book Section*, January 11, 1930, p. 1.

20. (Boston: Lothrop, Lee & Shepard Co., 1905), pp. 40–41.

21. Letter, HLW to Leon Wilson, June 11, 1936. WP.

22. Letter, HLW to Leon Wilson, August 17, 1936. WP.

23. Letter, HLW to Leon Wilson, December 13, 1937. WP.

24. Letter, HLW to Hamlin Garland, September 24, 1903. Garland Papers, University of Southern California.

25. *Historic Waterways: Six Hundred Miles of Canoeing down the Rock, Fox and Wisconsin Rivers* (Chicago: A. C. McClurg and Company, 1888), p. 89.

26. Letter, HLW to Leon Wilson, December 18, 1934. WP.

27. Information from Albert Lawson.

28. Oswald Garrison in *The Iowa Falls Sentinel*, reprinted in *The Oregon Independent*, November 21, 1883.

29. Letter, May Wilson Miller to Leon Wilson, December 14, 1940. WP. Miss Alberta Pantle, Librarian of the Kansas State Historical Society, informs me that the 1883–1884 *City Directory* of Topeka lists Lester S. Wilson as "stenographer in the executive office of Governor George W. Glick."

30. Letter, HLW to Homer Croy, March 14, 1923. Owned by Homer Croy. See also Harry Leon Wilson, "A Good Humored View of a Small Town," *New York Tribune*, April 22, 1923.

31. *The Boss of Little Arcady*, p. 128.

32. Undated note in pencil on letterhead of the Saint Francis Hotel, San Francisco, where HLW says he had come for dentistry. The letter belongs to 1934 as he says he "turned 67 on May 1st." WP.

33. "Art for Red Gap's Sake," *Saturday Evening Post*, CXCV (December 16, 1922), p. 104.

Higher Education

As a little boy Harry sometimes wanted to be a railroad switchman when he grew up, for he thought running along the top of a rapidly-moving train the most fascinating job in the world. Later, under the influence of his reading in dime novels, he sometimes dreamed of becoming a detective, the scourge and terror of all evil doers; but more often he imagined himself winning glory as an author. This aspiration was natural, for both his father and mother prized books, and his father occasionally tried to write fiction. Whether or not any of Samuel Wilson's stories were ever published is uncertain, but the editor often read the manuscripts to his wife. In one of these narratives he made a character say, "Then I took a chaw of tobacco." When Harry overhead his father's words, he was puzzled because he knew Samuel hated tobacco. Finally, the boy concluded that writing was a fine game of "let's pretend." He himself read eagerly in Dickens, Bret Harte, and Mark Twain, and his secret hope was to follow after these masters.[1]

Harry was practical enough to realize that until he had proved he could write, he would need a steady, if less fascinating job, and so in November, 1884, when he was thrown on his own resources at the age of seventeen, he was thankful to get work as a stenographer in the Omaha offices of the Union Pacific Railroad Company.[2] There he performed his duties so faithfully that a year later he was promoted to a position in the Denver office at what was then considered a good salary—$75 a month, nearly double what he had been getting in Omaha. But he soon lost most of his enthusiasm for his work when shortly after arriving in Denver he discovered that $25 a month was to be taken out of his salary until the new typewriter he was using was paid for. When he vigorously protested this arrangement to his superior in Omaha that official replied he was "surprised and pained" that a man he had recommended should take such a narrow view. Harry answered that he was surprised and pained that the Union Pacific expected him to pay for its equipment. As a result, in December, 1885, he found himself jobless in Denver.[3]

He was not long out of work. Answering an advertisement in a Denver newspaper, he became secretary to Dr. Edwin Fowler, manager of the Bancroft History Company, one of the most remarkable businesses west of the Mississippi. Much has been written about this concern, and about its founder, Hubert Howe Bancroft, a San Francisco book dealer of Yankee antecedents, who had the magnificent idea of writing the history of the Pacific slope, including Canada and Mexico, and who in furtherance of his plan set up an assembly line designed to turn out volume after volume of his work, quickly and efficiently.[4] Surprisingly enough, Bancroft made a fortune from his "history factory," and what is perhaps still more surprising the quality of his machine-made product was fairly high. Scholars are greatly in his debt. But for his foresight and willingness to take risks, our knowledge of the history of the West would be much less complete than it is. He bought private papers, hired copyists to explore archives in California, Mexico, and Spain, assembled a library of over 60,000 volumes pertaining to the Pacific slope, and sent several agents, of whom young Harry Leon Wilson was one, scurrying throughout the West to take down the recollections of the pioneers. The materials Bancroft collected were valuable; after he was through with them, Reuben Gold Thwaites appraised them at $350,000, and in 1905 the University of California at Berkeley paid $150,000 for the lot.[5] Bancroft deserves credit for performing a needed service at the only time it could be done, a service which no one else had either the vision or the courage to attempt.

Unfortunately, the tapestry has another side. Bancroft was essentially a business man without any scholarly scruples either about signing his name to the writings of his assistants or about exploiting the vanity of the early settlers, some of whom were led to believe they must subscribe to his *History* in order to secure favorable mention in it. Moreover, many of the subscribers complained that when they signed the order they had no idea they were obligating themselves to take the entire set of thirty-nine volumes at a cost of up to ten dollars a volume, because the salesman had not specified how many books were in the set. One of those who protested most loudly was Leland Stanford, who as a patriotic gesture had agreed to take forty sets, under the impression that the work would run to only five or six volumes.[6] Incidents of this sort gave Bancroft a reputation for sharp practice throughout the West, but as Professor John Walton Caughey, his sympathetic biographer, points out, he probably did more good than harm. In part at least, the University of California's eminence in Western history was founded on the materials he collected.

Harry Leon Wilson in his later years said that the activities of the Bancroft History Company were merely "a benign form of literary racketeering,"[7] but he never denied he learned a great deal during his employment with them. Indeed, it is not too much to say that his work with Bancroft was Harry's

H. L. W. as editor of "Puck" in about 1894

Rose O'Neill (Courtesy of Leon Wilson)

substitute for college, and an excellent one it was. To be sure the curriculum was narrow, but it was thorough. It gave Harry a fine background in Western history and geography and a solid grounding in practical psychology. "That job was," he told his daughter, "my introduction to human nature."

As an agent Harry called on prominent oldsters and explained that Mr. Bancroft was engaged in writing the history of the western states in thirty-nine volumes and that he needed some facts about their lives for this great work. Usually the prospective victim would then vacillate and say, "Well, now really, there's nothing important for him in my life . . ." and Harry would come back with, "That's something Mr. Bancroft knows best sir; it is your duty to your family and posterity to see that the hard lessons you've acquired are not allowed to float away on the whirling stream of time; we must transfix them, sir; make them an enduring monument to *your inherent worth*." Next would follow a discussion of the oldster's life, how he went to school winters and worked on the farm summers, and what his experiences in the Great West had taught him. At the proper moment Harry would say, "Mr. Bancroft, of course, wants to know that you appreciate this great work," and flicking out an important-looking document reading, "In token of my high regard for the great work Mr. Bancroft is doing and the tremendous boon it will be to the Pacific Coast, I hereby subscribe, etc.," try to get him to sign.[8]

Harry worked with Dr. Fowler for over a year in Colorado during which time he was paid a salary of $50 a month plus expenses. Since most of the people they tried to interest were leaders in their respective communities, Fowler and Harry had to keep up appearances. Thus they stayed at the best hotels and were careful to dress well. For a boy who had always been forced to be extremely careful of his money, this experience of expense-account living was a revelation. Hearing of it, his relatives in Illinois shook their heads and sent him a lot of advice about saving money, which Harry told his children he was wise enough not to take. In Harry's view experience was the most valuable treasure a young man could garner. "I hope you don't save a dollar," he wrote when his son got his first job in Hollywood.[9]

During such spare hours as he was able to squeeze out of his labors for Bancroft, Harry tried to teach himself to write, using as models the short pieces in *Puck*, the leading comic weekly of the day. Hopefully, Harry sent one of his compositions, "The Elusive Dollar Bill," to the magazine. The piece, which was based on the difficulties Harry had once encountered in Denver when he attempted to exchange a silver dollar for a dollar bill pleased the editor, who sent him ten dollars for it and invited him to contribute more material of the same sort. The path to the fulfillment of his dream of becoming a writer now opened before him, and he energetically set about writing short items for *Puck* whenever he had the leisure. Characteristically, he was generous with the extra money his writing brought him. In a letter to his sister, May, he sent five dollars "for a dress for Ma."[10] He also reported that *Puck* had accepted "Her," a short burlesque he had written on Rider Haggard's story "She." He added

"Dr. Fowler wrote to me about a week ago from San Francisco. He wants me to come out there and go to Southern California with him—the situation will be permanent this time. I wrote him I would go for fifteen dollars per week and all expenses. So I may leave here for there in a month. He is a good man to be with and I think the work will do me lots of good in many ways.

"In the first place I am out of doors most of the time, and that makes it healthful. And then I will be seeing lots of interesting country and learning something all the time. Then too, I constantly have a desire to write about something and the country may give me some 'ideas.' Will be twenty years old the

first of next month and will be old enough to 'vote'
in a year. We have had perfect weather here all the
time. The grass became green before the middle of
March, and the trees are beginning to bud. Booth
(the actor) will be here next week."

The West was full of ghosts in the late eighties of the last
century. In a postscript to this letter Harry told May he had
attended a seance, and expressed his conviction that "spiritualism can't be all mind reading because they told me about
Ma's sister, described her and told me how old she was when
she died—when I didn't know she had ever had such a sister."
Harry, however, soon grew skeptical, when following the advice of one of the mediums he bet a week's salary on Drummer Boy, a horse that the medium's control, an old chief of
the Blanket Indians, said was a sure thing. "Drummer Boy
isn't in yet," Harry told his daughter in 1938. But his experience with the spiritualists was not a complete loss; it suggested the episode in which Bunker Bean learned from the
clairvoyant that he was a reincarnation of Napoleon.

Accepting Fowler's offer, Harry went out to California early
in the summer of 1887. This time, however, he did not work
on the *History of the Pacific States*, but on another Bancroft
venture, *The Builders of the Commonwealth*, a set of seven
volumes, consisting of the biographies of one hundred of the
leading citizens of California, that is the hundred of them
who were willing to pay from one thousand to five thousand
dollars for the distinction of appearing among the elite. As to
the value of *The Builders*, there is some difference of opinion.
Professor Caughey asserts that several of the biographies are
worth having, as the roster included "half a dozen governors,
half a dozen United States senators, a chief justice of the
United States supreme court, San Francisco's most distinguished vigilante, several railroad tycoons, a number of leading bankers" and so on.[11] On the other hand Major Horace
Bell, who regarded the entire biographical industry as a colos-

sal fraud, points out that a good many old gamblers, stock brokers, and shoddy real estate men were included.[12] Perhaps both Professor Caughey and Major Bell are right; they seem to be looking at the same people from different points of view.

For Harry Leon Wilson *The Builders* had at least this merit: the project enabled him to see California. He went first to San Francisco and immediately fell in love with the city. He was just twenty years old, had never been east of Oregon, Illinois, had never seen any place more impressive than Omaha or Denver, and so was ripe for adventure. "I lost no time," he told H. L. Mencken fifty years later, "in getting to the bar room of the Palace Hotel to see if the floor of same was truly set with silver dollars. Doubtingly I had long listened to that sensational tale and I found it true in all its incredible elegance. And the town itself! The flawless beauty of maidens to be passed on Market Street, beaming cordiality to the newcomer, the profusion of flowers erratically blooming at a season untimely by all sane standards—it made a rapture the years haven't staled. I get a bit of it back at every casual invasion of the town; even the taxicab drivers seem different to me.

"Some years after that debut I recall being asked if I hadn't found the fogs depressing. With annoyance I demanded, What fogs? and hotly declared that the air I there walked on had been invariably sunlit. It was not less than the Afternoon of a Faun. Debussy tells it all."[13]

After a short stay in San Francisco, he and Fowler went on to Los Angeles, a city he later disliked, but which then he thought romantic, since some of the old Spanish traces still survived. About a year and a half later, however, in July 1889, he left California and returned to Omaha where once more he found a job with the Union Pacific railroad, this time as secretary to Virgil G. Brogue, Chief Engineer. His duties in this position required him to travel a good deal over the area served by the railroad, and thus he added to his already extensive knowledge of the West. In 1938 he could not remember why he left the Bancroft Company, but thought it was probably "the result of some row with Fowler, an insufferably conceited ass, who was always overhearing some woman exclaim that he was the handsomest man she had ever seen."[14] Meanwhile Harry continued to write for *Puck* whenever he had any spare time. Most of his contributions were readily accepted, for he studied the magazine carefully, especially the stories of its editor, H. C. Bunner, a graceful writer, who though not a college man, loved Shakespeare, the British essayists, and Horace, which he read in the original.[15] Like most humorists he was sometimes sentimental, and in addition to his urbane accounts of the sunnier aspects of life in New York and its suburbs he was the author of that favorite of the school readers,

> "There was an old, old, old lady
> And a child that was only three."

Still Bunner knew when he was being sentimental and his best work shows the results of his close study of Maupassant and Sardou. He prized good manners and urbanity. Harry learned much from his pieces in *Puck*. "I read him religiously," he recalled in 1931, "slavishly tried to copy his happy turn of words and I did feel so good when achieving a phrase that might plausibly have been his—an occurrence not frequent, however. No other writer came at all near to filling this need of mine. I especially remember a quite brazen imitation of his 'Love in Old Cloathes' which I wrote and *Puck* happily accepted for publication, though sent off with violent misgivings."[16]

In its day "Love in Old Cloathes" was considered one of the most charming of American humorous short stories. Actually, it is merely a pleasant trifle, the humor of which depends upon the contrast between the setting—an Eastern suburb, perhaps Tarrytown—and the language, Bunner's version of seventeenth or eighteenth century English: "for when I 1st became sensible of ye folly of my Suite, I tooke to drynking and Smoaking, thinkinge to cure my minde, but all I got was a headache, for fellowe to my Hearte ache—A sorrie Payre!— I then made shifte, for a while with the Bicycle, but breaking of Bones mendes no breaking of Heartes and 60 myles a Daye brings me no nearer to a Wedding" and so on.[17] Harry's "brazen imitation" of this was "An Amateur Lover," which, though it may lack some of the charm of Bunner's story, seems to have more point. It sets out to ridicule Puritanism by deriding an overly pious eighteenth century youth such as Harry imagined Jonathan Edwards to have been. The passage in Edward's *Personal Narrative* about how that spokesman for an angry God delighted in thunder storms is skillfully parodied: "Often I walked abroad in Solitary places in ye fields and forests. I saw ye trees and clouds, and drew fm them a strange and keen sense of ye Presence of God—Thunder and Lightnying I fd exceedg Entertaining, as being God's method of Hinting at Hys direful wrath agst sinners."[18] Because the priggish hero can't stop thinking of a young woman whose "hair is of a Wanton Curliness" and the nape of whose neck "is as white as anie snow," he concludes she is a witch.

Harry had been writing for *Puck* for over five years when in February 1892, the magazine offered him a job in New York as Bunner's assistant at a salary of $25 a week plus payments for any contributions he might write. Though the salary was less than he was getting from the Union Pacific, he accepted the offer with alacrity. Until then he had never been east of Chicago and he regarded New York as the great world, the Mecca of every ambitious spirit.

In the nineties there flourished in the metropolis three humorous magazines of national circulation—*Life, Judge,* and *Puck.* Of these *Puck* was the oldest, the most firmly established, and the most influential, occupying a position in America analogous to that occupied in England by *Punch. Puck,* however, was no mere imitation of its English counterpart. Its front and back covers as well as the gaudy double-page spread in the middle were drawn by cartoonists like Joseph Keppler, Bernard Gillam, F. Graetz, and Frederick Opper, all of whom belonged to the German school of caricature; and in tone and subject matter the jokes, lively paragraphs, light verse, character sketches, parodies, short stories, and editorials which *Puck* set before its readers in great profusion was almost aggressively American. The Columbian Exposition at Chicago in 1892 from which the magazine issued a special daily edition was an indication that both the country and the magazine were beginning to flap their wings and crow. Harry, however, did not get to the Fair; he worked on the regular New York edition in *Puck's* imposing red brick home on Houston Street, where over the front entrance a gilt statue of the little fellow himself flaunted the legend, "Lord, what fools these mortals be!"

If the Bancroft History Company was Harry's college, *Puck* was his graduate school. There he learned the trade of literary comedian under a distinguished faculty, nearly every one of whom was a fully accredited N D (Noble Drinker), a degree for which, so Malcolm Cowley tells us, writers used to toil as hard as students are said to for the Ph. D., and which signified that the holder could consume large quantities of alcohol without showing any effects.[19] Though Harry tried hard to emulate the triumphs of his teachers, he never quite succeeded. He did well enough, however, to be accepted as one of the gay and talented group of choice spirits among which he surprisingly found himself. Almost immediately they elected him treasurer of The Cloister, a club which met at 20 Clinton Place and included among its members such lights as Bunner; Emil Carlsen, the artist; Alfred Q. Collins, a well-known portrait painter; James L. Ford, dramatic critic for the *New York Herald*; John G. Dater, financial writer for the same newspaper; R. K. Munkittrick, humorist and member of *Puck's* staff; and E. W. Townsend, the creator of Chimmie Fadden. As treasurer Harry's duties included collecting the dues, paying the rent ($75 a month), and supervising the French cook, who in return for giving a dinner for fifty cents was allowed to live in the building and make what he could out of the bar. Since the cook was a good one, every member was expected to drink enough to encourage him. When in a gallant effort to perform this obligation a weaker brother would collapse, a stronger one would take him home, "place him on the door mat, ring the bell, and flee."[20]

Several years later The Cloister furnished the details for The Monastery, a Bohemian club described in Harry's novel, *Ewing's Lady*. Like The Cloister the fictional club was located in "a dingy-fronted brick house in Clinton Place," a little off Broadway. The hall was bare and echoing but the rooms were broad and lofty "with stained floors, mantels of gray marble, and rich old doors of polished mahogany framed in white casements." The walls were covered with plain grayish-brown paper on which the artistic clubmen had made charcoal sketches of monks struggling against the temptations of the world. "Over the mantel in the first room a pink-fleshed nymph in simple garb of chef's cap allured an all but yielding St. Anthony with one of the club's dinner menus held before his hunger-lit eyes. On a panel to the right of this a befuddled lay brother, having emptied a flagon of wine, perched on the arm of a chair and angled fatuously in a jar of mocking goldfish. . . . To the left, Brother Hilarius furtively ignored his breviary as he passed a gay *affiche*, from which a silken-limbed dancer beguiled him with nimble, worldly caperings." (pp. 109–110)

For Harry the nineties were a golden era, when life was full of stimulating experiences in what was then truly "little old New York," a city without subways, automobiles, trucks, or tubes under the rivers, with only one bridge—Brooklyn Bridge —and whose tallest building was a twenty-three story structure in Park Row. His salary climbed rapidly and so did his standard of living. Developing epicurean tastes, he became an authority on fashionable restaurants like Delmonico's and Rector's as well as on such Bohemian ones as Mouquin's, Buchignani's (a favorite resort of Stephen Crane and Frank Norris), Maria's in McDougall Street and Koster and Bial's in Park Place.[21] He got passes to the theaters and could speak persuasively of the merits and defects of Lillian Russell, Fanny Davenport, Mrs. Fiske, Weber and Fields, and Harrigan and Hart. He was able to dress as stylishly as Richard Harding Davis's Van Bibber, and one day while riding on a crowded street car he found himself in a predicament which might well have taxed the good nature of that ideal of the gilded youth. Unnoticed by Harry, a pickpocket lifted another passenger's watch. A detective, seeing the theft, moved forward to make the arrest, whereupon the guilty man dropped the watch in Harry's pocket. Thinking Harry an accomplice, the officer arrested both men. Harry protested vigorously, but to no avail. At the station when he gave his name as "Harry Wilson," he was greeted with shouts of laughter. Greatly puzzled, because he was ignorant that that was the name apprehended pickpockets usually gave, he had some difficulty in establishing his innocence. The next day, however, he received an apology and a cordial invitation to lunch from the Commissioner of Police, Theodore Roosevelt—proof of the high regard in which politicians held the members of the staff of *Puck*.[22]

Harry's almost boundless energy made him a valuable assistant to Bunner. In addition to performing such chores as reading hundreds of unsolicited jokes, a most melancholy duty, he contributed a large amount of both prose and verse to the magazine, some of it under his own name, some pseudonymously. In 1894 he collected a dozen of his short stories which had appeared there in a small volume called *Zig Zag Tales*, a title suggested by Bunner because their settings alternated between East and West. They reveal a light touch and the ability to manage the sort of surprise ending later associated with O. Henry. Typical of them is "Father Cortland's Vacation" in which a minister traveling incognito in the West gets into a poker game and from it emerges with enough money to pay off the mortgage on his church. Nor was O. Henry the only popular writer whose techniques and subjects Harry and other contributors to *Puck* anticipated. Almost five years before George Ade began making fun of the morality of the McGuffey readers in the first of his *Fables in Slang* (September 1897),[23] Harry had parodied McGuffey in a sketch entitled "Somebody's Grandmother," published in *Puck* for January 4, 1893:

"It was a cold, raw day in the latter part of the month of March, and the rain, which had but lately fallen made the crowded streets of the great city of Boston very damp and slippery, indeed.

"At one of the most crowded crossings stood a group of newsboys who had gathered to dispose of their papers. Suddenly one of their number exclaimed:

"'Hi there! Get on to her ringlets.'

"The object of his impulsive remark was an elderly lady in old-fashioned attire, who stood upon the opposite side of the street, vainly seeking an opportunity to stem the tide of travel. She carried in one hand a wicker basket, and in the other a reticule; both of quaint design. About her wrinkled face hung the gray curls which had elicited the above comment.

"The boys turned their eyes upon the old lady, and were engaged in making unmanly remarks about her peculiar appearance, when a tall, neatly-dressed lad of some ten years, with a bright, manly look in his clear hazel eyes stepped from their midst and said, in clear, ringing tones:

"'Shame on you, boys, for thus ridiculing one whose advanced age renders her oblivious to current prejudices in the matter of dress! Here, George Morton, hold my papers, while I assist the ancient but worthy dame across the street.'

"Henry Splitlog, for this was our hero's name, was quickly

at the old lady's side," . . . and so on. Evidently the wits of the nineties thought McGuffey fair game.

So faithfully did Harry toil for *Puck* that in 1896 when Bunner died at the age of forty, he succeeded him as editor. His salary was then $80 a week, and as he wistfully recalled in 1938, "in those days you could do a lot with $80."[24] One of the things Harry did was to rent a seven-room bachelor apartment at the corner of West End Avenue and One hundredth street for some sixty dollars a month. Money went much further in those days. A good derby hat cost three dollars; men's shoes of good quality five; men's suits at Wanamaker's ranged from ten to fifteen; and eighteen dollars would buy a splendid overcoat. For a dollar and a half one could enjoy a fine Sunday evening supper with music under the ornate bronze gas chandeliers of any of the better hotels. The top price for theater tickets when Sarah Bernhardt was the attraction was three dollars; one could see less famous actresses from an orchestra seat for a dollar and a half. Harry did not believe in saving money; he lived opulently, as befitted an editor of *Puck*. "It was pleasant," he told his son in 1938, "to feel you were somebody at thirty."

Full of confidence, Harry decided to venture forth upon the dangerous sea of matrimony. He had met the woman he wanted for a wife as early as 1886 in Boulder, Colorado when he was barely nineteen and working for the Bancroft History Company.[25] She was Wilbertine Teters, the daughter of Colonel Wilbert Barton Teters, a gold mine operator, whom Harry was trying to interest in having his biography written by Bancroft. Colonel Teters would have nothing to do with the scheme, but he liked the young agent so much that he brought him home to dinner, where Harry met Wilbertine, who was then a student at the University of Colorado. She was twenty years old, had red-gold hair, fair complexion, gray-green eyes, and a figure like Lillian Russell's, and Harry was certain she was the most beautiful woman he had ever seen. Soon after their first meeting he took her rowing on Weisenhorn's Lake, where he asked her to marry him. He was a handsome stripling whose presence in the town had caused considerable excitement among the beauties of Boulder, probably because he stayed at the Brainard Hotel and wore a splendid light-tan suit. Wilbertine's refusal on the ground that she didn't love him must have been a shock. Hoping to change her mind, he wrote to her frequently after he left Boulder, but with no success. Yet even after she refused to answer his letters and had married Charles Worden, the owner of an English language newspaper in Mexico City, he could not forget her. When in 1897 he learned that her husband had died and that she and her small daughter were then living in Denver, he resumed his courtship, writing nearly every day, telegraphing often, frequently sending her violets, and imploring her to come to New York for exciting and fashionable events like the horse show. Eventually, he wore her down, and yielding to his pleas, she came East, though with some misgivings. They were married in the Chapel of the Angels in the then fashionable Saint Michael's Church at 99th and Amsterdam Avenue on February 15, 1899.

Because Harry was unable to take time off from *Puck* just then, instead of a honeymoon he merely brought his bride home to his bachelor apartment. There Wilbertine became rather lonely until Harry suggested she send for Helen, her little daughter, then about four years old. The presence of the child did a great deal for both of the adults. Harry, who had a real understanding of children, was enchanted by Helen to whom he liked to tell stories about how Santa Claus would come into their apartment through the dumb-waiter as they had no fireplace. He often bought her expensive dolls and other toys and he enjoyed taking her and her mother to expensive restaurants like Rector's and Delmonico's, where Helen could survey the passing show from a highchair. There was a piano in the apartment and Harry and Wilbertine and their friends liked to gather around it and sing such numbers as "I've Been Working on the Railroad," "Louisiana Lou," and "Wheeling Together." The bicycle craze was then at its height; Harry bought wheels for Wilbertine and himself, and taught her to ride. Every Sunday afternoon they would join the fashionable crowd which pedaled up Riverside Drive as far as Grant's Tomb, Wilbertine wearing a smart but rather daring bicycling costume consisting of a divided skirt which reached to her ankles.

Wherever he was or whatever else he was doing, Harry seldom ceased thinking about *Puck*. On Saturday mornings he would shut himself off from household interruptions in the small library, where, garbed in his white terrycloth bathrobe and fortified by a box of cigars and a friendly thirst-quencher, he would tap out his amusing and satirical editorials for the magazine.[26] In those days he took a keen interest in civic affairs, such as the celebration for Admiral Dewey when that hero returned from Manila, and he was tireless in attendance at forums where all sorts of progressive ideas from the single tax to free love were being discussed. He took Wilbertine to one of these at the Waldorf so that she might meet Elbert Hubbard, who for a time impressed Harry as an advanced philosopher. Later, Harry decided it was Hubbard's baggy pants and cotton umbrella that made him think the Fra an intellectual. In his editorials he attacked graft, protectionism, the Chinese Boxers, free silver, yellow journalism, the Presbyterians, and Kaiser William. He approved of Dr. Lyman Abbott's liberal pronouncement that even cynics might get into heaven, and Emile Zola's stand in the Dreyfus affair.

Harry dressed well, preferring dark brown or gray suits. A fine physical specimen with thick brown hair, square jaw, generous mouth, and cold gray eyes, he was quite susceptible to women, many of whom were naturally attracted to him. He had long since discarded the standards of the Midwest for those of the Bohemians with whom he was associated on *Puck*.

Wilbertine's ideals and values, however, were still Victorian. She liked a few of Harry's friends such as Charles Davis, the brother of Richard Harding Davis, and Paul Leicester Ford, the author of *Janice Meredith*; but for most of them she had a positive aversion. She was a patrician, the grand-niece of General Lewis Cass, who had been a candidate for President of the United States in 1848. When gossip reached her that Harry had been attending parties on the yacht of the notorious James Gordon Bennett, which lay at anchor in the Hudson, only a block or so away from the apartment, and that on these occasions he had been too attentive to a woman who lived just around the corner, her pride would not allow her to remain with Harry and she returned to Denver where she had no trouble in getting a divorce.

The failure of this marriage hurt Harry; perhaps it left a permanent mark. As he never spoke of this part of his life, his children knew nothing of it until April 1938 when in their efforts to straighten out his affairs after Wilson had had a stroke they ran across some reference to Wilbertine among his papers. He was then a sick man, and when they asked him for information he angrily told them it was no concern of theirs. Believing they had a right to know, they wrote to Tarkington, who replied, "That question you asked me. Can't shed much light, though I've searched my memory. I *think* I recall that *Rose* once spoke of the first, as if H. L. had told her. Something like this: He'd been in love with her as a boy—teen sweethearts—then she 'married another,' and had a little girl who became the apple of H. L.'s eye. Adored the child and for years kept a photograph of her on his desk—Then the mother, the 'old sweetheart' lost her husband, and H. L. to be near the *child*, married the widow. It wasn't a success and I think that Rose didn't know why; but there was a divorce— H. L. kept his photograph of the little girl though.

"To me, he made one reference. About 1908 we were writing a play called 'Foreign Exchange,' and fishing for the right name for the chief girl, I suggested 'Jennie' or 'Lucy'—one of those two I *seem* to recall, and he said casually, 'It won't do. I used to know somebody of that name.' Faint smile, not bitter, not very relishing, either, explained what he meant; we *laughed* perfunctorily and went on with the search.

"That's *all*—'there isn't any more.' I'm pretty sure it was all that Rose knew. H. L. always knew 'all about' *me*—he was for months with me at my old home here, with my father and mother; but when he left, one day to go to see *his* mother, that was the first and last I ever heard of her. When we were arranging, in the spring of 1908, to *return* to Paris, where we both kept apartments, he mentioned that he was taking his brother along—so I found he had a brother—and two weeks before we sailed he asked me to cancel the SS reservations I'd made for Rose, which was all the news I had from him that he and Rose were separating. . . .

"We had, I suppose, a 'tacit agreement'—he'd tell me anything in which I was concerned or that interested him to tell. There wasn't any grimness in his habit of personal reticence; though people who didn't know him well often thought him grim."[27]

Unquestionably the divorce saddened Harry. For years Wilbertine had meant to him about what Daisy Fay had meant to Scott Fitzgerald's Gatsby—success, status, romance. When she and her little daughter dropped out of his life his job at *Puck* lost its zest, and everything in New York turned flat and stale.

He longed to return to the West, but since editorial jobs comparable to his place on the magazine did not exist there, he saw no way of leaving the city.

At this point W. C. Gibson, the art editor of *Puck*, whose cubicle was next to Harry's, mentioned to him that one of *Puck*'s most popular illustrators, Rose O'Neill Latham, was also having domestic trouble and that she had gone home to Missouri to get a divorce. "At this news, Harry recalled, "I pricked up my ears and began to dream."[28] A gifted, ebullient young woman, Rose was worth dreaming about. She had grown up in Omaha, where her father, William Patrick O'Neill, a book dealer, more interested in the contents of his wares than in their prices, had a hard struggle to provide for a family of six children. His great hope was that Rose might become a Shakespearean actress, but when she began to show much more talent for drawing than for the stage, he encouraged her natural bent. Self-taught, she was producing illustrations which newspapers were willing to buy when she was scarcely fifteen.[29] In 1893 at the age of eighteen for further training she had gone to New York, where she lived at a convent of French nuns, one of whom always accompanied her on trips to editorial offices when she tried to sell her drawings. She didn't sell many, and after a few months in the city she rejoined her family in the Ozarks, where in the meantime they had homesteaded a three-hundred-acre farm. Three years later, now married to Gray Latham, she returned to New York and again laid siege to the magazines; this time she was successful and publications like *Puck, Truth*, and the *Cosmopolitan* gave her more work than she could do.[30] Unfortunately, Latham turned out to be an unworthy husband and Rose was compelled to divorce him.

Soon after her return to Missouri, Rose began to receive lively, delightful letters and gifts of books from an anonymous admirer. She had no idea who this mysterious person might be. She did not think of Harry, for she had known him only casually from having seen him on her trips to the *Puck* office, and it was some time before she noticed that whoever wrote "Cartoons and Comments," Harry's page in *Puck*, had a style similar to that of the letters.[31] After she received her divorce, she returned to New York, where she found it hard to believe that the Harry Wilson who wrote the letters was the same person as this stern silent editor whose square head and face gave the effect of a granite wall. Nevertheless they became engaged. According to Orrick Johns, Rose had the gift of awakening hidden abilities in many frustrated and incomplete people.[32] Certainly, she helped Harry at a critical point in his career. He wanted desperately to leave New York and to free himself from the editorial grind. The only way he could do this, he believed, was to write a novel, and so under the inspiration of Rose he set energetically to work on *The Spenders*, the story of how a family made rich by the mines of the West threw away a fortune in New York. At that time and for some years afterward, the attempts of wealthy but crude miners from the mountain states to invade New York society caused much comment, for in those days Americans, even those of no social pretensions, liked to discuss the doings of the rich. In 1899 a lively topic of conversation was the one-hundred-and-thirty room house of white granite which Senator William A. Clark of Montana proposed building at the corner of Fifth Avenue and Seventy-seventh Street, a model of which was on view at the Architectural League. Six years later *Collier's* hailed the completion of this monstrosity with an ode by Wallace Irwin:

> Senator Copper of Tonapah Ditch
> Made a clean billion in minin' and sich,
> Hiked for Noo York, where his money he blew
> Buildin' a palace on Fift' Avenoo.
> 'How,' sez the Senator, 'can I look proudest?
> Build me a house that'll holler the loudest—'
>
> Forty-eight architects came to consult,
> Drawin' up plans for a splendid result:
> They'd give 'im Art with a capital A. . . .
>   .   .   .
> Pillars Ionic
> Eaves Babylonic
> Doors cut in scallops resemblin' a shell:
> Roof wuz Egyptian,

Gables caniptian,
Whole grand effect, when completed, wuz—hell.[33]

The miner's children in Harry's story built no houses in New York, but they succeeded in illustrating the old saying "from shirt-sleeves to shirt-sleeves in three generations." Wastrels, they are cured of their foolishness when they return to the West, and go to work for a living.

In the light of Harry's later development one character in the book is especially noteworthy. Uncle Peter Bines, a salty old prospector, who had known the contemporaries of Fremont, Kit Carson, Harney, and Bridger, represents a type which Americans have admired from the days of Poor Richard to those of Will Rogers. In the first quarter of the present century this figure appeared often in our popular literature; among its embodiments are David Harum, Old Gorgon Graham and Scattergood Baines. Harry drew the type over and over again—as Daniel Voorhees Pike in *The Man from Home*, as Sharon Whipple in *The Wrong Twin*, and as Ben Carcross in *Lone Tree*. Always a rustic, always humorous, sometimes melancholic, usually rich, the image represented a national ideal. Of it we have no reason to be ashamed. As Ferner Nuhn has pointed out there are worse ideals than this "agile, sober, joking folk god;" the humorless fanatic on horseback has caused a great deal more grief in the world.[34]

Uncle Peter's sturdy common sense often clashes with the effete notions of his grandson's eastern friends. Interrupting their chatter about the inferiority of American wines, he declares, "Well, you see, young men, we're not much on vintages in Montana. Whiskey is mostly our drink—whiskey and good spring water—and if our whiskey is strong, it's good enough. When we want to test a new barrel, we inject three drops of it into a jack-rabbit, and if he doesn't lick a bull dog in six seconds, we turn down the goods. That's as far as our education has ever gone in vintages." To him New Yorkers, not Westerners are provincial. Of a certain Easterner he observes,

"I just couldn't help snickerin' over his idee of God's own country. He thinks God's own country is a little strip of an island with a row of well-fed folks up and down the middle, and a lot of hungry folks on each side. Mebbe he's right. I'll be bound, it needs the love of God. But if it *is* His own country, it don't make Him any connysoor of countries with me." (p. 336)

Many people admired Uncle Peter, among them William H. Crane, a well-known character actor who had won success in the role of David Harum. Dramatizing *The Spenders*, he scored another triumph as Uncle Peter in 1903. Harry had created a valuable literary property. Indeed *The Spenders* sold so well that one month after publication, the publishers felt justified in giving Harry a $2000 advance on it. As soon as he received this money, he resigned his job on *Puck* and on June 7th married Rose in a civil ceremony in Jersey City. After a honeymoon of several weeks in the mountains of Colorado and a visit to Harry's mother in Illinois, they went to live with Rose's family in the Ozarks. In his old age Harry told his son that two of the greatest thrills of his life were getting to New York in 1892 and getting out of it ten years later.[35]

Notes

CHAPTER TWO
Higher Education

1. C and L's Notes.

2. Letter, Mr. Edwin C. Schafer to the author, July 25, 1958.

3. C and L's Notes.

4. John Walton Caughey, *Hubert Howe Bancroft, Historian of the West* (Berkeley: University of California Press, 1946), pp. 99–117.

5. *Ibid.*, p. 363.

6. George T. Clark, "Leland Stanford and H. H. Bancroft's 'History'; A Bibliographical Curiosity," *Papers of the Bibliographical Society of America,* XXVII (1933), p. 21.

7. C and L's Notes.

8. This paragraph is based on C and L's Notes and "Smith's Biography," a sketch HLW published in *Puck,* April 6, 1892.

9. Letter, HLW to Leon Wilson, December 18, 1934. WP.

10. Letter, HLW to May Miller, Denver, April 15, 1887.

11. Caughey, p. 316.

12. *On the Old West Coast* (New York: W. Morrow & Co., 1930), pp. 288–289.

13. Carbon copy of letter from HLW to H. L. Mencken. April 16, 1937. WP.

14. C and L's Notes.

15. Brander Matthews, *The Historical Novel and Other Essays,* (New York: C. Scribner's Sons, 1901), pp. 166–167.

16. "H. L. on Bunner," *Saturday Review of Literature,* XXI (March 16, 1940), p. 19.

17. The Stories of H. C. Bunner, Second series, (New York: C. Scribner's Sons, 1916), p. 2.

18. *Puck* (August 23, 1893).

19. *The Literary Situation* (New York: Viking Press 1954), p. 206.

20. James L. Ford, *Forty-odd Years in the Literary Shop* (New York: E. P. Dutton & Company, 1921), pp. 253–254.

21. Albert Parry, *Garrets and Pretenders* (New York: Covici, Friede, 1933), p. 90; also information from Helen Worden.

22. Letter, Theodore Roosevelt to HLW, August 29, 1895. WP.

23. Bergen Evans, "George Ade, Rustic Humorist," *American Mercury,* LXX (1950), pp. 321–324.

24. Clipping. *San Francisco Call,* December 25, 1925. WP.

25. This paragraph is based on information from Helen Worden. Interview April 7, 1963.

26. Letter, Mrs. Luellen T. Bussenius to the author, July 26, 1957. Mrs. Bussenius was Wilbertine's sister. She visited the Wilsons in New York soon after their marriage.

27. Letter, Tarkington to Charis and Leon, April 28, 1938. WP.

28. Maude M. Horine, *Memories of Rose O'Neill* (Copyright 1954 by the author, but no place or publisher given), p. 15. Copies of this thirty-five page pamphlet may be purchased from the author in Branston, Missouri.

29. *Ibid.*, p. 8.

30. *The Reader*, IV (November, 1904), p. 698.

31. Horine, p. 15. Miss Lee O'Neill in an interview in March, 1958 told the author that "Meemie," Rose's mother, was the first to discover the similarity in style between the letters from Rose's anonymous admirer and Harry's page in *Puck*.

32. *The Time of Our Lives, the Story of My Father and Myself*, (New York: Stackpole Sons, 1937), pp. 257–258.

33. Grace M. Mayer, *Once Upon a City* (New York: The Macmillan Company, 1958), pp. 39–40.

34. *The Wind Blew from the East*, (New York: Harper & Brothers, 1942), p. 8.

35. Letter, HLW to Leon Wilson, December 16, 1935. WP.

The Man From Home

BONNIEBROOK, THE O'NEILL HOMESTEAD, was a rambling, fif-teen-room house, located deep in the Ozarks, in a rugged glen far off any main road, and nearly fifty miles south of Spring-field, Missouri. Rose and Harry, who occupied the entire sec-ond floor, made themselves comfortable there, importing from New York luxuries like Harry's favorite brands of coffee and tobacco; hiring a staff of mountain people to fetch and carry for them; and transforming an unusually large room into a combination studio and study furnished with books, pictures, Navajo rugs, and a Steinway piano.[1] They were fairly well-off, as *The Spenders* sold well and the magazines took all the illustrations Rose could do. This gifted woman who as a little girl had lived in a tumbled-down shanty on the top of a clay bank in Omaha,[2] was deeply loyal to her family and deter-mined to do everything she could for her younger brothers and sisters, seeing to it that James and Clarence were sent to Creighton University in Omaha and Miss Lee to a school in Baltimore. Harry was glad when they were away, for their almost incessant laughing and giggling annoyed him, espe-

cially in the early morning. He swore that they laughed in
their sleep, that they woke up laughing, that they were bar-
barians who had never heard that Lord Chesterfield had laid
down the rule that a gentleman never even smiles before
10:00 a.m. Still, on the whole, Harry got along very well with
his in-laws. Rose's mother—Meemie—was fond of him, and he
and old Mr. O'Neill enjoyed scoring off one another. Once in
an unguarded moment Harry told his father-in-law a legend
current in the Wilson family to the effect that in England a
fortune awaits the American Wilson who can prove his de-
scent from a British aristocrat named Wolfson. Thereafter,
Mr. O'Neill treated Harry as though he were a member of
the nobility, hastily arising whenever his son-in-law entered
the room and ostentatiously offering him the best chair. This
Harry would accept with immobile face, as if it were his by
divine right.[3]

During his years at Bonniebrook Harry worked hard trying to discover the sort of fiction he could do best. Hoping
that he would never again have to take an editorial job, he
stuck to his desk every day from eight in the morning till four
in the afternoon. Then he relaxed with some vigorous exercise such as playing bounce-ball off the side of the house,
hiking, or hunting. Small game was plentiful in the neighbor-
hood and Harry liked to surprise the family with the rabbits,
squirrels, and wild turkeys he brought in. In the evenings he
and Rose often read together. Hazlitt and George Meredith
were among their favorites, but one day amid Mr. O'Neill's
stock of books, which was scattered over most of the house,
they came upon some stories by a writer hitherto unknown to
them, a man named Joseph Conrad, whom Harry immediately
pronounced a genius.[4]

The three novels Harry wrote at Bonniebrook—*Lions of the
Lord* (1903), *The Seeker* (1904), and *The Boss of Little Arcady*
(1905) are not among his best, but they are interesting as illustrations of the trial-and-error process by which he discovered

where his real talent lay. Though they were written for money, it would be unfair to call them pot-boilers. Harry always had an exalted idea of the vocation of the popular author, and at this period his ideal was H. G. Wells, a novelist who taught as well as entertained. In each of these early books, Harry also tried to teach. The lesson he set out to implant in *Lions of the Lord* was that a fanatical religion can make a fundamentally good man commit murder. During his youth in the West he had listened to many thrilling tales about the "Destroying Angels" of Brigham Young, a band of men who were supposed to take revenge upon Gentiles who mistreated Mormons, and in preparation for his book he read a great deal about the massacre of some one hundred twenty non-Mormon emigrants at Mountain Meadows in southern Utah in 1857, said to have been instigated by the Saints. Joel Ray, the central character in Harry's novel, takes part in this outrage. A sincere Mormon, who had witnessed the terrible persecutions of his co-religionists in Missouri and Illinois, and participated in the trek across the plains to establish a New Jerusalem in Utah, he is persuaded that he ought to become a Destroying Angel. Later, he realizes he has been duped and suffers agonies of remorse. Woven in with this theme is a sentimental love story involving the Gentile ward of Ray and two rival suitors —a prince of the Mormon church and a manly cowboy.

Lions of the Lord sold fairly well, and the reviewers, none of whom seem to have had anything good to say about Mormonism, were generally favorable. "No stronger, more suggestive story dealing with the psychic effects of religious dogmas and doctrine has appeared in recent years," said the influential *Independent*.[5] Harry's next book, however, was to teach him that it was one thing to attack a then rather unpopular sect like the Mormons but quite another to attack organized religion in general. *The Seeker*, the thesis of which was that in an era of Darwinism and general scientific enlightenment ministers and priests had to be hypocrites, was widely condemned as an attempt to do what Harold Frederic and other writers had done better several years before.[6] H. G. Wells, however, to whom Harry sent a copy, found the story informative. "The Seeker," he wrote, "is a novel after my own heart, just the sort of travel and happenings among views and beliefs that I like to write myself. And to an English reader it's tremendously illuminating. Extraordinary creature an American Episcopalian bishop must be, a thing against nature like a Yorkshire Buddhist or a Swiss Mohammedan. What else have you done that you'd like me to read?"[7]

The extraordinary creature which interested Wells was the villain of Harry's melodrama, Bernal Linford, a religious careerist, who though trained as a Presbyterian minister becomes for business and social reasons an Episcopalian rector, and finally a Roman Catholic priest, after having lost his wife to his brother, a humanist. Though a caricature, he is quite as convincing as Sinclair Lewis's Elmer Gantry whom he anticipated by twenty-three years. Harry's summaries of Bernal's sermons, of which the following is a fair sample, are as amusing as anything in Lewis's book and do much to compensate for the overly-sentimental love story: "Hardly was there a dissenting voice in all St. Antipas that Sabbath upon the proposal that this powerful young preacher be called to its pulpit. The few who warily suggested that he might be too visionary, not sufficiently in touch with the present day, were quieted the following Sabbath by a very different sermon on certain flaws in the fashionable drama.

"The one and only possible immorality in this world, contended the speaker, was untruth. A sermon was as immoral as any stage play if the soul of it was not Truth; and a stage play became as moral as a sermon if its soul was truth. The special form of untruth he attacked was what he styled 'the drama of the glorified wanton.' Warmly and ably did he denounce the pernicious effect of those plays that take the wanton for a heroine and sentimentalize her into a morbid attractiveness.

The stage should show life, and the wanton, being life, might be portrayed; but let it be with a ruthless fidelity. She must not be falsified into a creature of fine sensibilities and lofty emotions—a thing of dangerous plausibility to the innocent" (p. 208).

Harry's next book, *The Boss of Little Arcady* (1905), is a sentimental evocation of life in a small town as it might have been in his boyhood rather than as it was. In structure the novel consists merely of a string of farcical episodes involving familiar village types—an editor, a shyster lawyer, a Civil War veteran with an empty sleeve, a southern belle, a lady reformer from New England, a faithful Negro servant, and a barefoot boy who is fascinated by dime novels. No villagers were ever so idyllic as these; they represent an attempt on Harry's part to refashion some of the people he had known as a child closer to his heart's desire, and the general effect is similar to that which James Whitcomb Riley achieved in his poems. Yet the story sold fairly well and a good many rather discriminating people liked it. In 1912 Jack London told Harry he thought it was his favorite novel, a little later Barton Currie called it "a fine contemporary record" and in 1922 Hildegarde Hawthorne still thought it "a much bigger and more human book than *Main Street*."[8] Furthermore, the theme of the novel—the need to idealize life—is more subtle than anything in Riley, though Harry's way of bringing it in may remind one of Riley. The Civil War veteran, speaking of his dog, says, "Sometimes in half a doze he breathes a long, almost human sigh of despairing comprehension, as if the whole dead weight of his race's history flashed upon him; as if the woeful failure of his species to achieve anything worth while, and the daily futilities of himself as an individual dog were suddenly revealed. In such instants he knows, perhaps, that there is little reward in being a dog, unless you cheat yourself by believing more than the facts warrant. But presently he is up to dash at a bird, with a fine forgetfulness, quite as startled by the trick of flight as in his first days. And I, envying him his gift of credulity, weakly strive for it" (p. 288). What is this gift of credulity but the "sophisticated" philosophy of "as if," that is "the determination to act as though we still believe the things" which former ages really believed but which we know are delusions—the attitude that such philosophers as Bertrand Russell, Unamuno, and Santayana recommend to their disciples?[9]

Often in his fiction Harry expresses a somewhat subtle point of view in homely terms. In an interview in 1930 he confessed that he had always been a teacher, but that he had tried to keep the didactic intention from interfering with the story.[10] In the three novels just considered he did not always succeed in doing that, but they do reveal a progressive mastery of his craft and a growing awareness that the comic mask fitted him better than any other.

As a former editor and as a professional author Harry followed developments in the magazine business closely. The years during which he lived at Bonniebrook fall within the era which has been called "the golden age of magazine publishing."[11] In 1907 more than forty general magazines, most of them selling for ten cents, were published in New York alone—all of them competing for a share in a rapidly expanding market. The interests of this flourishing industry were promoted by a strong trade organization, the Periodical Publishers Association, which every spring sponsored a convention where authors and editors were brought together in some pleasant resort hotel. The 1905 meeting at Lakewood, New Jersey, was an important milestone in Harry's literary career, because there he shared a suite with David Graham Phillips, George Horace Lorimer, and Booth Tarkington.[12] The association thus begun with Lorimer was later to ripen into friendship as the editor came to regard Harry as one of the most dependable contributors to the *Saturday Evening Post*. Equally important was Harry's relationship with Tarkington, who greatly admired *The Boss of Little Arcady*. The two men had met in New York as early as 1902 and in the summer of 1903 Tarkington and his wife and Harry and Rose had spent some time together at Cos Cob.[13] Now in the intervals of wining, dining, and general merrymaking at Lakewood, Booth and Harry comparing notes, decided that in view of the success of *Monsieur Beaucaire* and *The Spenders* on the stage, writing plays might be more profitable than writing novels. Accordingly, they decided to go abroad together and collaborate as playwrights.

Tarkington and Harry, accompanied by their wives, sailed for Italy on the *Koenigen Luise* on September 9, 1905.[14] After an uneventful crossing, a brief stop at Naples, and a short excursion to Pompeii, the two couples settled down on Capri, where they had rented the Villa Quattro Venti from Elihu Vedder, an American artist, famous for his illustrations in the *Rubaiyat*. Life at the villa, which is located on the saddle of the island half way between Capri and Anacapri and commands an excellent view of the Bay, was delightful. There were no irksome domestic chores because the place came fully equipped with a staff composed of a chef, a gardener, and the gardener's wife, who served as maid. The dreamlike landscape, the trees—orange, olive, lemon, palm—the old Roman ruins, the sparkling Mediterranean, the healthy, shapely, barefooted, peasant women, who frequently broke into song as they walked along the winding, climbing road, combined to suggest to Harry that he was living on the stage of a musical comedy in which Tarkington and he had buffo parts. Both men were fond of practical jokes. One of their favorite pranks whenever they heard Americans were coming to the island was to lock Tarkington in the tiny jail at the foot of the campanile and shock their compatriots with a detailed account of the crimes which had brought disgrace upon him.[15]

Before long, two other amiable American couples, the Julian Streets and the Lawrence Mazzanovichs (Mazzanovich illustrated Tarkington's books) joined the American colony, and there were also several interesting visitors to the villa, among them George Ade, Norman Douglas, and William Graham, the painter. Often Booth and Harry spent the afternoon playing tennis with their guests.[16] One of these, an exceptionally good player, was the Englishman whom Julian Street in his reminiscences called Peveril Brydge. Booth and Harry had met Brydge on the boat coming over, and soon after their arrival he entertained them lavishly at the Hotel Quisisana. Everything about him, his manners, his taste, his fine leather luggage, and his valet indicated he was a gentleman of the first water, and so one evening after they had been on the island about two months Harry suspected nothing when Brydge's valet appeared at the Villa Quattro Venti with a note to him complaining that Brydge had been greatly embarrassed by Signor Serena, who had barred him from the dining room till he had paid his bill. Brydge had all along supposed the bill paid, but his man—so the note said—had let it run and Brydge was now in great difficulty because today was Friday and the fellow who took care of his business in London and who always promptly cabled funds as needed had left for the week-end. Would Harry be kind enough to tell Signor Serena to be civil in the interim? Harry, ever loyal to his friends, most decidedly would. Hastily penning a note to Signor Serena, he expressed his astonishment that a friend of his should be subjected to such discourtesy and added that any further harassment of Signor Brydge would result in Harry's withdrawing his patronage from the Hotel Quisisana. Within the hour a note arrived from Signor Serena to the effect that he would never have imperiled his relations with a patron of Signor Wilson's distinction, never even have mentioned the bill had he known that Signor Wilson was Signor Brydge's guarantor. If Signor Wilson would but write but the merest line indicating such was the case, the hotel management would be more than satisfied. Again Wilson obliged. A few days later Brydge and his valet quietly slipped out of Capri leaving Harry responsible for a hotel bill of nearly a thousand dollars.[17]

Though Harry could ill afford to lose that much, he took his medicine stoically. What vexed him most about the affair was the opportunity it gave Tarkington to score off him. "You must understand, Hank," said Tarkington in the manner of King Henry addressing the scapegrace Hal, "that over here sharpers don't wear big black mustaches and loud clothes and diamonds the way they do out West. Don't you think that till you catch up on things I'd better take care of your money for you?"[18]

Tarkington found he could not work on Capri, but Harry, who seems to have been able to write anywhere, completed *Ewing's Lady* there, working mostly at night. The two couples separated before Christmas, when the Tarkingtons because of Louisa's approaching confinement left for Rome where modern medical care was available.[19] The Wilsons remained at the villa until late in April when they rejoined the Tarkingtons in Paris and the partners finally got to work on their playwrighting.

Before Rose and Harry left the island, Vesuvius erupted, a sight which Harry told Tarkington "made one of Pain's Coney Island spectacles look like the fourth of July celebration [which] the small son of a cautious father has with three ten cent squibs—lava flowing down the sides of the mountain, solid columns of flame a thousand feet high from the crater, reflected miles above the smoke, a continuous rain of gold fire, and all imaginable doings in color."[20]

In the same letter Harry announced the completion of *Ewing's Lady*, a full-length serial he hoped to sell to the *Century Magazine*, of which Robert Underwood Johnson, a friend of Tarkington's, was co-editor. When Johnson refused the story, Harry sold it to *Ainslee's*. Later, Harry came to regret ever having written it at all, and certainly it is one of his poorest books. There are some vivid passages describing Bohemian

life in New York as Harry had known it during his days at
Puck, but the plot and the characters are as unreal, as theatrical as footlights and grease paint. The strangest aspect of
the whole performance is that a humorist of Harry's gifts
would overlook the opportunities for burlesque inherent in
an absurd fable about a young painter from the West who on
coming to New York falls into the clutches of a villain out to
revenge himself on the boy's parents by destroying the career
of their son. Perhaps Harry in preparation for his venture into
the drama had been reading too many popular plays.

Summer found Harry and Rose settled in an apartment at
246 Boulevard Raspail in Paris. The Tarkingtons were then
living at Champigny-sur-Marne, a dozen miles away, but
Booth and Harry dined together frequently at the Taverne du
Pantheon, where their fondness for practical joking soon became legendary. At dinner there one evening they were interrupted by a young Frenchman with a spade-shaped beard,
who politely asked if he might sit with them to improve his
English. To introduce himself he showed a hunting license,
signed in facsimile by the French secretary of agriculture.

"H. L.," said Tarkington, "allow me to introduce the Minister of Agriculture."

"Oh," said Wilson suspiciously, "you're quite a young man
to be Secretary of Agriculture."

"Oh, no," the Frenchman explained, his name was the name
at the top. It was just that the Secretary's name was on all
hunting licenses.

"Well," said Wilson, deadpan, "we understand you now ad-
mit you're not the secretary, but why did you misrepresent
yourself in the first place?"

Then the man grew excited. "Before I would misrepresent
myself to you who were so kind to permit me to sit at your
table, I would cut my throat!" he sputtered, drawing a finger
across his throat.

"No, no," said Harry, sadly shaking his head, "if you're

really sincere in being sorry for what you've done, don't cut your throat; just cut your beard."

At that the Frenchman suddenly realized that he was being hazed, but delighted at the good humor of the joke ordered drinks, and the three men passed a most enjoyable evening.[21]

In the spring of 1906 a certain magazine publisher from New York visited Paris. A circumspect bachelor, he was rumored to have carried on while aboard ship a mild flirtation with a chorus girl. When he arrived at the Wilsons' for dinner, he discovered to his great embarrassment that the actress had been invited also and that Harry was apparently laboring under the belief that the dinner was to announce the publisher's engagement to the lady.[22]

In September 1906 Harry and Tarkington finally began the first draft of *The Man From Home*, a play they had planned for a long time, but the actual writing of which they finished in about five weeks. Originally intended for David Warfield, who refused it, then offered to Nat Goodwin, who also turned it down, it was eagerly accepted by William Hodge, who was just then beginning to attract notice as a character actor.[23] Tall, red-haired and deliberate, Hodge was the Will Rogers of his generation, and like Rogers he did not need to act the part of a conservative provincial, astute, small-town American, for he was the thing itself.[24] In his early teens he had run away from his home in Albany, New York, to join a theatrical company touring the villages of Pennsylvania, and from small parts with this and similar companies he had worked his way up to such roles as Freeman Whitmarsh in James A. Herne's *Sag Harbour* and Stubbins in *Mrs. Wiggs of the Cabbage Patch*; but his great opportunity came when George Tyler, the producer who had bought *The Man from Home* from Tarkington and Wilson, offered him the role of Daniel Voorhees Pike, a Kokomo lawyer.[25]

For actor, producer, and authors the play turned out to be a sensational money-maker, netting six hundred thousand

Helen Cook (Photo by Weston)

H. L. W. at the Bohemian Club Grove, California, in 1919.

dollars in a five-year run in New York, Chicago, and on the road and paying both Tarkington and Wilson an average of two hundred dollars a week for the entire period.[26] After a try-out in Louisville, Kentucky, it opened at the Studebaker in Chicago on September 29, 1907, where it set a record of 375 performances; then Tyler brought it into New York to the Astor,[27] where to the great disgust of the metropolitan critics, it ran for over a year before going on tour.

The success of the *Man from Home* kept Tarkington and Wilson writing plays for the next three years. In that period they turned out five more plays. Though none of these was able to repeat the triumph of the *Man from Home*, all of them except *Foreign Exchange* were profitable. Yet, though the theater put Harry on Easy Street, it is probably fair to say that he never regarded playwrighting as anything more than a lucrative business. That he let other writers dramatize his novels, never attempted to write a play alone, never collaborated with any one except Tarkington may suggest that Tarkington was the partner most responsible for the success of their ventures. But this reasoning does not hold in view of Tarkington's statement: "I can write plays," he said, "but I could not have written *this* play nor half of it, without his collaboration."[28] "Our method of collaboration," said Wilson in an interview some years later, "is almost primitive. One or the other of us has an idea that will serve as the basis of a plot; we meet and talk it over. We decide upon the general course of the story, and take turns in telling each other that story in the simplest form possible.

"When we have it in a compact and tangible form we chop it into chunks or scenes. Then we discuss the characters and some of the principal details, both of us taking notes, and then we are ready to call in a stenographer. In the case of a dialogue between two characters we each take one and act out our scene, while the stenographer jots down the dialogue in shorthand.

"Of course, I don't mean to say that we rattle it right off, for it often takes a long time to get a speech to sound real. When we have gone through the play in this way, we make the poor stenographer read it to us, and bombard him with corrections and alterations. When he types the whole thing and turns it over to us, we each go through it separately, revising and correcting, and then read it through once more before we have a clean copy made for the manager's perusal. You can very well see how the identity of individual passages is lost in this process."[29]

In the *Man from Home* the shrewd and witty lawyer from Kokomo travels to Italy where he succeeds in preventing his wards, two foolish but rich young Americans, from marrying titled but cheap foreigners. Tarkington later said that when he and Harry made Pike say things like "I wouldn't trade our State Insane Asylum for the worst ruined ruin in Europe—no sir, not for hygiene and real comfort," they thought the audience would be amused at his aesthetic standards and laugh tolerantly at them while they sympathized with the common-sense view he took of his wards' wish to marry predatory Europeans.[30] When instead of laughing the audience applauded Pike's boasting thunderously, Tarkington asserted he was completely surprised. Apparently, he thought the miscalculation was due to the manner in which Hodge played the part, and according to Hodge's daughter, he was furious with the star. Wilson, however, she says, was quick to see that this was the only way it could be played. "He was co-operative at every point to point up the humor and satire of the 'Title Search' abroad. . . . Father invariably chuckled when he spoke of Mr. Wilson. He also did everything he could at every opportunity to see that Mr. Wilson got the credit he deserved as the co-author of 'The Man from Home.' "[31]

The reason for the great success of *The Man from Home* is apparent. Pike was a character with whom the provincial American could identify. In those horse-and-buggy days the differences between city people and country people were much sharper than in our industralized, homogenized, suburbanized era. Those Americans—by far a majority—who lived outside of the large cities were incredibly isolated. Railroad service was infrequent, the automobile was still "a rich man's toy," roads were dusty in summer and almost impassable in mud season, and except in sections fortunate enough to be connected by trolley lines, ten miles was considered a long distance.[32] The movies were only in their infancy, radio and television were as yet unheard of; and the shows put on in the "Opera House" or town hall meant a great deal to folks whose lives were pretty monotonous. Often these people had endured the slurs of supercilious Easterners who regarded any one who lived west of the Hudson as a tobacco-chewing rustic or bucolic clown. In Pike they saw a sturdy Westerner outsmarting the snobs, just what each of them wished he might do. Indeed Tarkington and Harry must have realized that the *Man from Home* was a contribution to "the American rural drama," a genre now obsolete, and then unknown outside of the United States, which included such classics as "The Old Homestead," "Way Down East," "The County Fair," "The County Chairman," "Shore Acres," and "David Harum." In all of these plays the figure of a shrewd American—usually a Yankee—is put up to be laughed *with* and not *at*. Even the name "Daniel Voorhees Pike" suggested such associations. Hearing it, many of the audience would remember Daniel W. Vorhees (1827–1897), an Indiana politician who because of his commanding figure had been nationally known as "the tall sycamore of the Wabash" and they would tend to associate Pike with a man from Missouri.[33] William Hodge, then, showed good judgment in keeping irony out of the part.

In later years Tarkington became more and more sensitive about what he considered Hodge's bumptiousness, and when he revised the play for a revival in 1925 he told Tyler to take care not to make Pike "a braggart who pretended to a sicken-

ing false humility, insulted helpless puppets and was offensive
without intermission. There was some of this in the writing,
but it became awful as he [Hodge] worked in his improve-
ments."[34] Pike, Tarkington saw as "a decent person . . . *really*
modest, but competent, shrewd, humorous, American—con-
fused and troubled by Europe, yet seeing his way through
and conscious (as an American) of 'no social inferiority'." As
for Hawcastle, he was no villain. "Do him," Tarkington advised, "a little as Henry James in his early period would have
done him," by which he meant a fine person who would not
want to take a mean advantage "but felt himself *pushed* into
it." Almeric, too, Tarkington thought, should be no stage
Englishman but "a little early H. J." Harry approved these
changes and Tarkington's proposal that they share 60 and 40
and after the first ten thousand fifty-fifty.[35] The revival, however, failed, for the world had changed a good deal since 1907.

When *The Man From Home* became a hit, Nat Goodwin,
who, as we have seen, had refused the part of Pike, asked
Tarkington and Harry to write a play for him. *Cameo Kirby*,
which opened in Columbus, Ohio, November 16, 1908, was the
result.[36] It is the story of a Bret Harte-type gambler, who in
ante-bellum days wins a plantation from the leading lady's
father in order to prevent the planter's losing it to another
card sharp. Before he can give back the property, however,
the planter commits suicide. In the end the virtuous Kirby
exposes the villain and restores the property to the heroine.
At first the play faltered, perhaps because Goodwin was too
old for the part, but when the lead was given to Dustin
Farnum, whose handsome eyes and winning smile had made
him the idol of matinee girls throughout the land, it became
successful on the road, though not in New York, where after
opening at the Hackett on December 20, 1909, it lasted only
twenty-four performances. Yet quite apart from the contribution of Farnum, the play had popular appeal; it was filmed
at least three times in the silent pictures, and in 1945 Twen-

tieth-Century Fox thought enough of it to pay $20,000 for the sound rights.[37]

Though *Foreign Exchange*, the next Tarkington and Wilson effort was a failure, lasting only from September 26 to October 15, 1909 at the Grand Opera House in Chicago, it reads well and might have succeeded had the right actress for the part of Miss Nancy Baxter been found. Miss Baxter, a naive American girl, the victim of her mother's mania for social climbing, has married into what she thinks a glamorous aristocracy. As the wife of Victor de Savergne, a profligate with a strange code of morals, she is so unhappy that she decides to run away, and the action ends with her successful escape with her child to a port on the English Channel.

While *Foreign Exchange* was failing in Chicago, *Springtime*, a play the partners wrote for Mabel Taliaferro, was being tried out in Philadelphia at the Garrick. On October 19, 1909, Frederic Thompson, the producer, brought it into the Liberty in New York, where it had a successful run of seventy-nine performances. Miss Taliaferro was a winsome, appealing, fanciful young woman with somewhat the same warmth and charm movie-goers later associated with Mary Pickford. Unfriendly critics said she couldn't act and that the play itself succeeded because Booth and Harry were writing for an audience which liked to recall "their days of schoolday passion, puppy love, handclasps, and change of finger rings";[38] less jaded commentators felt that the playwrights had given Miss Taliaferro a difficult part which she was able to make convincing. The action takes place in Louisiana during the War of 1812 and the heroine, a carefully brought-up French girl, falls in love with one of Andrew Jackson's troopers. When he leaves to fight the British, she follows him until turned back by the officers. The next morning when she returns home, her father, thinking she has disgraced the family, disowns her. She seeks refuge in the church, where while she looks on, her father lights candles to signify her "death."

On top of this she hears that her lover has been killed. Overwhelmed by her troubles, she loses her mind temporarily, but she regains it when her lover returns safely from the fray and her father forgives them.

While *Springtime* was doing a good business at the Liberty, Otis Skinner was having a fairly good season, first on the road, and after January 3, 1910, in New York at the Garrick, with *Your Humble Servant*, another Tarkington-Wilson play. Though most of the metropolitan critics thought the piece too sentimental, the *New York Times* was enthusiastic over the character of Lafayette Towers, a barnstorming actor of the old school, comparing him to Pickwick and Wilkins Micawber, but concluding that on the whole the conception probably owed most to Mark Twain's Colonel Sellers, who always dreamed of prosperity in the future. Like Sellers, Towers always thinks he's on the point of scoring a glittering success, even when his road company is stranded and because of his age he is unable to get another engagement. His greatest hope is to make a star of the young and beautiful Margaret Druce, who has been his ward since childhood. When because of his coaching, Margaret becomes a great lady of the theater, she rejects an aristocratic suitor for Lafe who she realizes has loved her all along.

Your Humble Servant, which was successfully revived by the Pasadena Playhouse in 1943,[39] is really very good theater. The first act, a play-within-a-play, takes place behind the scenes of Tower's production of Richard III at Weedsport, New York, with the sheriff, who has come to attach the company's luggage as soon as the Shakespearean performance is over, seated on Lafe's trunk. This agent of the law fancies himself a critic, and during the intervals when Lafe is "off-stage" tries to give the old thespian some friendly tips about the sort of drama which succeeds in Weedsport—"a play like 'Broadway Belles,' with a cute little blonde for a leading lady." His devotion to the drama, however, does not prevent his seizing Lafe's trunk at the end of the act.

In his memoirs Skinner gives an account of how the play was written.[40] He had, he says, long wanted to portray "an actor of the old bad school—one of those simple fellows given overmuch to 'sound and fury' whose mental horizon was bounded by back-drops, wings and footlights," and because of the great success of *The Man from Home* he commissioned Tarkington and Wilson to write a comedy featuring such a character. The first draft they assured him would be ready by July 1908, when Skinner planned to be in Paris. It was, but when he went to Tarkington's apartment near the Luxembourg Gardens to see what they had done, his spirits dropped. As Tarkington began the reading, Harry Wilson, "a rather sensitive man, warm in his friendships, and impatient in contradiction" started to pace up and down the room like a caged lion, making suggestions which began mildly enough but which soon grew so harsh that Tarkington answered back in kind. Skinner tried to inject a few ideas of his own with the result that by the time the session ended the three men were in the midst of a loud, confusing wrangle. That night at his hotel Skinner was unable to sleep, wondering whether or not he would have a play. Early the next morning, however, the two playwrights arrived at his room—"buoyant, hopeful, smiling, declaring that last night's session had been one of harmony and understanding." Evidently Skinner thought he had witnessed Booth and Harry's usual method of collaboration; but in view of the partners' love of practical joking it is not unlikely that they were trying to see whether their simulated outbursts would take in an experienced actor.

If I Had Money, the fourth Tarkington and Wilson play to be produced in 1909, opened at the Grand Opera House in Chicago on October 17th with Madge Carr Cook as the star. It recounts the adventures of Mrs. Jim, a worthy widow who keeps a boarding house for miners in Yellow Dog, Montana.

When gold is discovered on her claim, she sets out for New York, hoping to hobnob with the four hundred. There, her partner, Jim Blake, who has silently and hopelessly admired her for years, rescues her from the wiles of an aristocratic rake. Though the play contained some amusing situations, it was taken off after a run of less than two weeks. Evidently the public was at last tiring of variations on *The Man from Home*.

In the summer of 1910 Tarkington revised the script extensively, shifting the scene from New York to Paris and changing the title to *Getting a Polish*. The revised version, starring May Irwin, a popular singing comedienne, was fairly successful, both on the road and in New York. Miss Irwin, a plump Mrs. Jim, made a good many jokes about the discomforts of life in high society—tight shoes, tight lacings, and so on—and these coupled with her malapropisms and songs put the play over.

During the period when he worked as a playwright—that is, from 1906 through 1910—Harry drank more than was good for him, and this weakness as well as his alternating moods of silent gloom and affable jollity had much to do with the failure of his marriage to Rose. The widely-circulated story of their parting—how Harry, growing tired of her baby talk, warned Rose that if she ever said "wosies" for roses again he would divorce her, and how one fatal morning in Paris when he was suffering from a hang-over, he got up from the breakfast table and walked out of the apartment and her life forever, because she, entering with an armful of American beauties, exclaimed, "Mell my pitty, pitty wosies"—may contain a grain of truth, but scarcely more.[41] The fact is that it was Rose who left Harry and not the other way about. After their return to America in September 1907, she decided she could not go on living with a man whose moods were as uncertain as Harry's, and so she went home alone.[42] Later, she said that though she never wanted to go back to Harry and had never understood him, she loved him as long as he lived. Harry was certainly no model husband. In the spring of 1907 without telling Rose where he was going, he left her in Paris while he and George Tyler, the theatrical producer who had bought *The Man from Home,* toured Italy, Sicily, and Northern Africa in Tyler's automobile. Today, this trip sounds tame enough, but in 1907 automobiles were still a novelty, and Tyler, an enthusiast whose talk was full of strange terms like magneto, carburetor, chain drive, and transmission, and whose idea of fun was to race the boat train from Paris to Le Havre, had already demolished several cars. Harry seems to have enjoyed the trip through Italy, but in north Africa Tyler gave him so many thrills as they raced along the coast at sixty miles an hour that on reaching Tunis Harry invented some urgent business requiring him to take the next boat for France, leaving Tyler to complete the trip alone. The *Paris Herald* for May 21st reported him back in Paris with many interesting stories about his journey into places where most of the natives had never before seen an auto. What Rose thought of these stories, the newspaper didn't say.

On the other hand, Rose too had her vagaries. Among the Wilsons' neighbors on Capri was Charles Caryl Coleman, a painter whose pictures of Vesuvius in eruption were once highly esteemed. After serving in the Union army in the Civil War, he had settled in Capri, where he stayed for the rest of his days. There he had bought the convent of Madre Serafina, which he remodelled and rechristened the Villa Narcissus, a Moorish-like structure with white-tiled floors, twisted pillars, and an inclosed court, where roses and fig trees flourished. Now a lonesome old man troubled by debts, he appealed to Rose, who suggested to Harry that they give "Cinquecento Charlie," as Coleman was called, a small pension. Harry indignantly refused. Rose helped Coleman anyway, certainly later and probably then too. At any rate Coleman left the villa to her in his will, though in order to get a clear title she had to pay, so she told Harry, some $15,000 on Coleman's debts.[43]

For three years after Rose and he separated, Harry lived an unsettled, peripatetic life, having his mail forwarded from the Players Club. For example, in April 1909 he was in Pinehurst, North Carolina, on a vacation, in May in Indianapolis working with Tarkington, probably on *Your Humble Servant.* In June both men were in Paris, where they kept separate apartments; and in September, back in New York. Sometimes Harry would join one or another of the touring companies for a few days. Often Tarkington and he had several plays in rehearsal simultaneously, and this necessitated a good deal of travel.

By the spring of 1910 the playwrights began to see that they were working a dead-end street, for the taste of theatergoers was changing rapidly. Influenced by Shaw and Ibsen, even provincial audiences wanted "realism," that is plays like Eugene Walter's *The Easiest Way* and Edward Sheldon's *The Nigger.* Then too, the complaints of metropolitan critics that Tarkington and Wilson cynically refurbished "the stale conventions, the worn-out melodramas, and petty bathos" of yesterday in order to pocket the money of "the rustic mob" began to annoy both men.[44] Furthermore, Tarkington's heavy drinking and his resultant marital troubles made writing difficult. Accordingly, the partners decided to abandon playwrighting, and for the time being to separate, Tarkington returning to Indianapolis and Harry to the far West.

Harry spent the summer of 1910 in the Canadian Rockies with a pack train. The vacation freshened his spirits so much that he decided to make his home permanently somewhere on the Pacific Coast. "I washed Broadway, the Players, the Lambs, and all New York from my system," he said in 1930, "and I didn't go back."[45] Nevertheless, in the summer of 1918 and the fall of 1919, Harry did bring his family to Kennebunkport in order to work with Tarkington on another series of plays.

During these sessions the partners wrote *Up from Nowhere, Tweedles,* and *How's Your Health?* The first of these was intended for Otis Skinner, but he refused it. When put on in New York in September 1919, the leading part, that of a rough and ready self-made millionaire who had fought his way up from the slums of New York, was given to Norman Trevor, whose British accent did little to make the character convincing. Like *The Man from Home,* the story involved the winning of a young woman by an older man. The millionaire, puzzled at his son's wish to marry into a family of impoverished aristocrats, determines to court the girl himself in order to show the boy she's only a fortune hunter, but when she proves to be a prize, he marries her. Alexander Woollcott called the whole affair "languid"[46] and the public agreed with him.

Tweedles, though it did not reach the stage until April 21, 1923, when it was tried out in Cleveland at the Ohio Theater, was much more successful. With a cast including Ruth Gordon, Cornelia Otis Skinner, and Gregory Kelly, it lasted for ninety-six performances in New York at the Frazee. The plot exploits the antipathy between the natives of a New England village and the summer people. Julian Castlebury, the scion of the aristocratic Philadelphia Castleburys, falls in love with Winsora Tweedle, whose folks run the village antique shop; but the parents of both boy and girl oppose the match. Alexander Woollcott thought the scene in which the Castleburys discover that the Tweedles don't think Julian good enough for them a splendid piece of humor. What the production proved was that there was still a public for wholesome comedy without any deep psychological or sociological implications.

How's You Health? was not produced until the depression year of 1929 when it ran for forty-seven performances in New York at the Vanderbilt. It is an entertaining farce about a hypochondriac whose physician, in the hope that song and merriment will make him forget his ills, gets him to attend a party. There the imaginary invalid has a delightful evening, but not in the way the doctor hoped. Through the power of suggestion he convinces all of the other guests, including the doctor himself, that they are dangerously ill. The idea is amusing and the carefully-chosen cast included Donald Brian of the original *Merry Widow* company and Roy Atwell, the stuttering comedian, but in December 1929 the public was in no mood for such nonsense; the depression was real, not psychological.

Long before the onset of the depression, "the road"—that is the provincial theater for which Tarkington and Wilson wrote —had virtually ceased to exist. People who lived in the small towns, the whistle stops, the jumping-off places, no longer depended on the Town Hall or Opera House for entertainment: they now had automobiles, bridge, radio, and movies. Furthermore, it became increasingly clear that to succeed in Louisville or Toledo a play had first to succeed on Broadway. Harry, realizing he knew nothing about writing for Broadway, wisely let Kaufman and Connelly dramatize *Merton of the Movies*, which with Glenn Hunter as the star, became one of the most successful plays of the 1922-1923 season. Throughout the twenties, he devoted himself to writing comic romances, a genre rather rare in America in his time but for which he had great talent.

Notes

CHAPTER THREE

The Man From Home

1. Letter, Rose O'Neill to HLW. Bonniebrook, October 11, 1936. WP: The author's notes of an interview with Miss Lee O'Neill, March, 1958.

2. *The Reader,* IV (November, 1904), 698.

3. Interview with Miss Lee O'Neill.

4. Rose O'Neill's unpublished autobiography. I am indebted to Professor Ralph McCanse for the privilege of reading this typescript.

5. *Independent,* LV (September 3, 1903), 2118–2119.

6. *The Dial,* XXXVII (1904), 211; *Bookman,* XX (1904), 48–49.

7. Letter, H. G. Wells to HLW, 17 Church Row, Hampstead, n.d., WP.

8. S. J. Kunitz and H. Haycraft (eds.), *Twentieth Century Authors* (New York: H. W. Wilson Co., 1942), p. 1530; *Fishers of Books* (Boston: Little Brown & Co., 1931), p. 129; *New York Times Book Review,* April 16, 1922, p. 16.

9. Joseph Wood Krutch, *The Modern Temper* (New York: Harcourt, Brace and Company, 1929), pp. 21–22.

10. Marion L. Starkey, "Harry Leon Wilson in California," *Boston Transcript,* Book Section, January 11, 1930, p. 1.

11. Burges Johnson, *As Much As I Dare* (New York, N. Y.: Ives Washburn, Inc., 1944), p. 227.

12. *Ibid.,* pp. 229–230.

13. Rose O'Neill's autobiography; Letter, HLW to Julian Street, June 27, 1932. Street papers.

14. James Woodress, *Booth Tarkington* (Philadelphia: Lippincott, 1954), p. 127. Rose O'Neill's autobiography.

15. Edwin Cerio, *The Masque of Capri* (London: Thomas Nelson and Sons, 1957), p. 112.

16. Woodress, p. 127.

17. Julian Street, "When We Were Rather Young," *Saturday Evening Post,* CCV (August 20, 1932), p. 44.

18. *Loc. cit.*

19. Woodress, p. 129.

20. Letter, HLW to Tarkington, April 14, 1906. TP.

21. Woodress, pp. 140–141.

22. Rose O'Neill's autobiography.

23. Woodress, p. 146.

24. Edwin Francis Edgett, "William Hodge," *Dictionary of American Biography*, XXI Supplement one (New York: Charles Scribner's Sons, 1944), pp. 411–412.

25. Mary B. Mullett, "This Runaway Boy Became 'The Man from Home,'" *American Magazine*, XCVII (April, 1924), 19; *Literary Digest*, XCI (October 16, 1926), 32.

26. Woodress, p. 146.

27. Albert Van Nostrand, "The Plays of Booth Tarkington," *Princeton University Chronicle*, XVII (Autumn, 1955), 17.

28. Woodress, p. 147.

29. Philip Loring, "The Craft of Collaboration," *Green Book Album* (May, 1910), 1010–1015.

30. Woodress, p. 147.

31. Letter, Martha Hodge Amory to the author. Undated.

32. Booth Tarkington, *The World Does Move* (Garden City, New York: Doubleday, Doran & Company, Inc., 1928), pp. 63–64.

33. See "sycamore" and "pike" in *An American Glossary*, ed. Louise Hanley (Madison, Wisconsin, 1939).

34. Tarkington's directions to Tyler on the revision of *The Man from Home* are in the Tyler papers in the Princeton University Library.

35. Information from Leon Wilson.

36. Throughout this chapter my information as to the out-of-town openings and New York productions of the Tarkington-Wilson plays is taken from Van Nostrand's tabulation of Tarkington's dramatic works, *op cit.*, pp. 33–39.

37. Woodress, p. 151.

38. *New York Dramatic Mirror* (January 15, 1910), p. 5.

39. Woodress, p. 153.

40. Otis Skinner, *Footlights and Spotlights: Recollections of My Life on the Stage* (Indianapolis: Bobbs Merrill Co., 1923), p. 299.

41. The story circulated among Wilson's friends as Woodress (p. 128) says, but it is an exaggeration. Rose and Harry returned to America together in September 1907. Tarkington knew nothing of their impending separation until

the spring of 1908 when he and Harry were planning to return to Paris. All he knew then was that "two weeks before we sailed he [Harry] asked me to cancel the SS reservations I'd made for Rose." (Letter, Tarkington to Charis and Leon, April 28, 1938. WP).

42. Rose O'Neill's autobiography. Also information from Miss Lee O'Neill. O'Neill.

43. Letter, Rose O'Neill to HLW, November 11, 1936. WP.

44. Percival Pollard, *Their Day in Court* (New York and Washington: The Neale Publishing Co., 1909), p. 285.

45. Starkey, p. 2.

46. *The New York Times*, September 9, 1919: "Mr. Tarkington and Mr. Wilson can people their pages with the most extraordinary and winning folk, but their plays take form before the footlights as concoctions singularly unreal and unconvincing."

Carmel

IN THE FALL OF 1910 Harry started down the Pacific coast seeking a place between the sea and the mountains where he could settle.[1] He found it at Carmel, then a writer's colony without paved streets, city water, or electricity, situated about 125 miles south of San Francisco on the edge of a pine forest facing the Ocean. Among the dwellers in this idyllic spot who soon became Harry's friends were Mary Austin, George Sterling, and James Hopper. Jack London, too, was a frequent visitor there, and he and Harry along with Sterling and Hopper had some great times hunting and fishing together.

At forty-five, thanks to his playwriting, Harry had achieved a measure of success financially, and when he found a tract of several acres of untouched forest, five miles south of the village and fronting the Ocean, he was able to buy it. There he built a large, comfortable, brown-shingled house which he named "Ocean Home." Joyfully, he wrote to George Ade, "I'm five miles in the country, surrounded by scenery and climate that are what people expect to find when they make for the Riviera; back yard full of wooded mountains and front yard, after you cross the rocks reaching clear over to Japan. The climate skins any other in California. If you ever come in midsummer I'd like mighty well to take you up to the Bohemian Grove for their Jinx. It's an experience worth travelling for and a week up there has been my yearly dissipation for three years. I've tried to get Tark out, but the poor lump believes the trip from Council Bluffs on is still made in wagons and interrupted by hostile Sioux."[2]

The event Harry describes was, of course, the summer encampment of the Bohemian Club of San Francisco at their Grove in Sonoma County, an occasion to which Sterling, Hopper, London, and Harry looked forward every summer. At these celebrations between six and seven hundred men would camp out for ten days or two weeks enjoying in Wilson's phrase "a he-time such as the world can't elsewhere produce."[3] After Sterling and London died, Harry joined a private camp in the Grove (of which there were many) called "Pebble Beach" to which Sam Blythe, the well-known political writer for the *Saturday Evening Post* also belonged.[4]

Pleasantly situated in Ocean Home, Harry decided he needed a wife to grace his new house, and so at the age of forty-five he began to court Helen Cooke, one of the prettiest girls in Carmel. Though only seventeen, she had been brought up among intellectuals and seemed older. As a child she had lived with her mother, Grace MacGowan Cooke, a successful writer for the women's magazines, in Helicon Hall, Upton Sinclair's socialistic community in New Jersey. After that institution went up in flames, the result—so the story goes—of janitor Sinclair Lewis' struggles with a counterrevolutionary furnace, Mrs. Cooke moved west, eventually settling in Carmel. Some time later, Young "Red" Lewis arrived there to become her secretary. The future winner of the Nobel prize was deeply smitten with Helen's charms and in 1909 went about chanting a sad pastoral entitled "A Fugitive Queen" which he had composed in her honor.[5] This failed to move her, but in 1912, at the age of seventeen, she married Harry Leon Wilson.

Helen was an imaginative girl, fascinated by Harry's stories of Paris and the great world. She saw Harry as a kindly and generous father-figure who might even be coaxed into taking her and their children to Paris. She did not realize that Harry wanted to stay put in Carmel, which to her was an isolated outpost cut off from civilization by a high ridge of mountains. Nor did she know what a complex, ambivalent personality this successful playwright was, how moody and silent he could be. Had she realized all of his disadvantages, had she been a bit older, Helen might well have hesitated before marrying him.

As for Harry, in spite of its stresses and strains and eventual failure, this marriage brought him the greatest happiness he was ever to know: a family of his own. On June 26, 1913 he jubilantly described to Tarkington the charms of his son, born the month before.[6] A few months later he wrote Julian Street, "Becoming a father hugely enlarges one's artistic appreciation. . . . I had some rooms in my noodle that had never been opened. There were wonderful things in them," and he went on to say he hoped the stork would be good to the Wilsons a few more times.[7] The stork obliged and Charis, a daughter, was born the following May.

In his earlier days at Ocean Home Harry's cup seemed to run over. Urging Street to visit him, the letter continued warmly, "I wish you could see the country here. It has all the scenic beauty of Capri, more to my thinking, because it has more variety, and the climate is the perfection of the Italian climate . . . what people expect to find there and miss seven times out of ten. It always requires a feat of calculation to know what season is here. My own place is unique as to location, a semi-circle scooped out of a mountain, five miles below Carmel, a precipitous and rocky front yard jumping off into the Pacific where there are more rocks, with the big white horses galloping in over them, all the way from Japan. My nearest neighbor is a painter a mile below me, here only for the summer. I have never grown tired of the place, never got enough of its beauty. The year round we are in the open air. We sleep on an open porch, the door of the living room is almost never closed and it's not easy to recall one disagreeable day. We've had two dry winters now, so I'm hoping for early rains, but even the rains are pleasant, honest rains that have to fight with the sun. . . . Back of the house I've just put in a swimming pool, 25x25, 8 feet deep. Also in the pool are 800 small trout that will soon have to be eaten of. . . . Out on the rocks are mussels (like your soft clams) and abalone, which you don't have. The abalone is a oneshelled beast as big again as your hand (variously) and three or four times as thick. He slices and fries, or makes chowder. He tastes like a chicken that ran away to sea and tried to be a lobster. The quail out in the back yard wake me up every morning. Also there are coyotes and jack-rabbits and wild-cats and mountain lions and deer, some farther away than others." And as if these attractions were not enough, Harry went on to say that Street would find plenty of inspiration for his writing in Carmel, a "literary and artistic colony," whose post office handles more rejected manuscripts "than any other of its size in the country." . . . "Naturally," he continued, the town, "is a hot-bed of gossip and all uncharitableness, with a 'forest threatre' complicated by amateur acting and amateur authorship, and very, very, funny. A book should be written about it, but I can get insurance on my house only for about two thirds of its value. Besides I want to live here."

Harry's happiness and contentment were soon reflected in his writing. He had always worked hard, but now since he had become the proud head of a family, his efforts seemed to have more point. At forty-five, he had not yet written his best, his most characteristic stories. All of these were turned out in his work room on the second floor of Ocean Home. There, dressed in an old bathrobe perforated with numerous cigarette holes, for he smoked incessantly as he wrote, he toiled eight or ten hours a day for months on end. The work room was bare except for his typewriter table and a larger table piled untidily with books, magazines, old newspapers, paste jars, match boxes, scraps of manuscripts, and playing cards. The cards were especially important, for when he was planning a novel he played endless games of solitaire, pausing from time to time to scratch down a note, consisting of a word, a phrase, or a sentence or two on a separate scrap of paper. Before he could begin a novel he had to have hundreds of these scraps. These he sorted out, just as a research worker does. Unless he went through this process he could not write. Nor could he even begin to compose until he had the entire story firmly in mind. In the planning stage he would often pace about the room, pausing now and again to look out over the pines and the rocks to the tossing Pacific.[8]

Once he had begun the first draft, Harry never stopped to rewrite but plowed on through to the end. Then he would revise. His invention was not especially fertile, and after he had finished a novel he would have to face the fear that he would never be able to write another. "It is my annual hell," he told a cousin.[9]

He worked slowly, and once in a letter to H. L. Mencken he regretted that he had not been trained on a big city newspaper where he might have learned to produce a large quantity of copy in a short time. "I doubt," Mencken replied, "that newspaper experience would have helped you to quicker writing. Undoubtedly it would have taught you how to slash out a lot of stuff in a few hours, but that stuff would be by no means the sort of thing you are doing now. In my own somewhat narrow experience, the value of writing seems to be in inverse proportion to the ease of writing. Whatever goes like pulling teeth tickles the eye."[10]

Harry first hit his stride in *His Majesty, Bunker Bean*, certainly one of the earliest studies of the badgered white collar worker, the "wage slave" in American fiction. Unlike Harry's previous novels, this one is focused on a single character from whose relations with the other characters the story develops. Bunker, a little man, pushed about by forces he can neither understand nor control, attempts to correct reality in his dreams. Uncertain as to whether his present state is a reward or a penance, he seeks the help of the Countess Casanova, who for three dollars tells him that he is the reincarnation of Napoleon Bonaparte. At first Bunker is delighted, but on second thought he fears that the boss' daughter, the flapper, (probably the first time this word was applied to a young girl in a novel) will discover who he really is and disapprove of the women in his karmic past as well as of his treatment of them. Fortunately, with the help of Professor Balthasar, who can penetrate the mist of time to a greater depth than could the Countess Casanova, he discovers that before he was Napoleon, he was King Ram-tah of Egypt, a monarch about whom the historians are silent, but who, Professor Balthasar assures him, was both virtuous and successful.

Bunker buys what Professor Balthasar tells him is his former body, the mummy of Ram-tah. This fetish gives him assurance enough to acquire on margin a large block of valuable stock and to marry the boss' daughter, but when he discovers the mummy is a fake, he goes through a difficult time until he learns to believe in himself.

Serialized in the *Saturday Evening Post* from October 12 through December 14, 1912, *Bunker Bean* was such a decided hit that Harry immediately became one of the inner circle of contributors to that magazine, and whenever Lorimer, the editor, came west on a vacation—which was nearly every year —he would have Wilson join him in a trip to some interesting place such as Palm Springs or the Grand Canyon. Lorimer realized that here was an author who could help him do what he thought the *Post* should do—"interpret America to itself."[11] Certainly in Bunker Bean thousands of office workers could see themselves. The little clerk, said Lee Wilson Dodd, is an embodiment of "the pathetic and childlike soul of America—and indeed of Man."[12]

H. L. Mencken was also enthusiastic about the story. "Oh, excellent Wilson," he exclaimed, "if I didn't tell you per private post, what a high old time I had over 'Bunker Bean,' then I do it now. The way you announced it, if you recall it, wasn't assuring. You gave me the idea that it was a hack job, done for the mazuma, and with little of you in it. But what I found was something I enjoy above everything—a first rate comic novel—save for 'Zuleika Dobson' the only good one in years! So I bawled through it during a happy evening, and next day began giving it to my friends. Imagine a book reviewer, steeped in graft, *buying* and giving away books! And yet I done it—and altogether, I suppose, a dozen times. What is more, I steered others to the shambles and made them leak. Such eloquence of the act transcends all the puny rhetoric of book reviews. I offer it in testimony of genuine joy."[13]

Though Bunker is a dream figure, a reincarnation of Jack the Giant-killer, his adventures are up to a point convincing, for they rest upon a foundation of autobiography. Like his hero, Wilson grew up in a small town, loved baseball, became a secretary to a railroad tycoon, and for a time was taken in by spiritualism. The germ of the novel, however, came to him from H. G. Wells' *Kipps*, a debt which he acknowledged by calling Bunker's home town Wellsville and by dedicating the book to the British author. Wells wrote Harry that he was "proud of his god-son."[14] Tarkington too sent his congratulations:

> 1100 North Penn St.
> Indianapolis
> Jan. 16, 1913

Dear H. L. —

I got an adv. copy of B.B. from D. P. & Co. and read it at a sitting (literally) which is "comment enough."

At the beginning, where you have present tense and strike back to birth, I felt threatened. That method has killed my reading of many a book—"Dern *him*, he's going to shoot his *planting* into me now" —but you so suddenly and immediately got hold of me with the manner of your ancient history that I was sorry when it was finished and you jumped back to N. Y.—a very well-timed jump since it left me anxious for more of the boyhood. The kid is universal, so it seems to be every he-reader's (and some she's too, I fancy) inner childhood. "Bricktop took my dime but gave me a 2-cent piece and a big cent. He said they were a good deal more than a dime, but weighed him down; he didn't want so much weight on his pocket." I hadn't a shell in my childhood—or that experience in *that way*, but I recognized it as true at once. Chubbin's double-nod is lovely—a great visualizer—Fine doings! Your illustrator's idea of Nap— on the verandah at "Claremont" or "Arrowhead Inn" seems to be eccentric—rather like a worm—and I noticed other queernesses, but, on the whole, thought him rather satisfactory; at least he doesn't *spoil* anything—doesn't keep you from seeing the people in spite of him. (I'm having my own troubles in that line just now.)

B. B. and the Flapper, her Daddy and (curiously) Grammer and Gramper remain the most distinct to me—I suppose you'll hear most of the Flapper and she is O.K. Of course, I see why you spoke of it once as a "sort of American Kipps" and ded. to H.G.W. but you certainly don't *owe* much to "Kipps"—any more than H.G.W. owed anything to "10,000 a Year." B. B. is glamoured all over with your whimsies and fun; you must have had a great time doing him. It's all distinctive; nobody else could have done it that

way; nobody else could have done it at all. You didn't
need to *sign* the canvas. Good luck to the selling![15]

Despite Tarkington, there are striking similarities between
the plots of Bunker and Kipps; each is an orphan, each re-
ceives an unexpected legacy; each dreams of cutting a figure
in the world. The great difference is that as an Englishman
Kipps suffers much more from snobbery than does Bunker,
who lives in a land where class lines are supposedly not hard
and fast. Significantly, the only one who objects to the flapper's marrying Bunker is her mother, a member of "one of the
oldest families in Omaha."

Any consideration of the evolution of the flapper in Amer-
can fiction will certainly have to take *Bunker Bean* into account, for if she did not make her bow in this novel (1912) she
made one of her earliest appearances. As Wilson pictured her,
she didn't drink or smoke; she was simply a healthy young
girl who played a good game of tennis, believed in woman
suffrage, and was out to get her man. Bobbed hair, hip flask,
and long cigarette holders were far in the future.

In *Bunker Bean*, equality is a subordinate theme; in Harry's
next novel, *Ruggles of Red Gap*,[16] it is dominant. Ruggles, the
valet of the Hon. George Augustus Vane-Basingwell, becomes
servant to the Flouds of Red Gap, Washington, when Senator
Floud wins him in a game of draw poker. Mrs. Floud had
taken a fancy to Ruggles in the hope that a good valet might
transform her backward brother-in-law, "Cousin Egbert," into
a gentleman or at least teach him what not to wear. And so
Ruggles comes to a land where one man is supposed to be as
good as another. At first he thinks the American spirit of
equality can only be "rather a ghastly jest" because "there
could hardly be a stable society in which one had no superiors,
because in that case one would not know who were one's in-
feriors," but as a result of his experiences he finally comes
to see that "Nature and the British Empire were at variance
in their decrees, and that somehow a system was base which

taught that one man was necessarily inferior to another."[17] Soon he was acclaimed social arbiter of Red Gap, a position which he accepted "only for the public good" and which he was willing to relinquish "as soon as a better fitted leader might appear." His policy in fulfilling the responsibilities of this office was to show Americans that "their equality should be more than a name."[18]

Like Mark Twain, Harry Wilson was aware that the American conviction that all men are created equal clashes with our inborn snobbishness. Twain, it will be remembered, noted that our hunger for rank and status clashed with our ideal of equality even in a primitive village like Hannibal, Missouri, where "everybody was poor, but didn't know it and everybody was comfortable, and did know it. And there were grades of society —people of good family, people of unclassified family, and people of no family. Everybody knew everybody, and was affable to everybody, and nobody put on any visible airs, yet the class lines were quite clearly drawn and the familiar social life of each class was restricted to that class. It was a little democracy which was full of liberty, equality and Fourth of July, and sincerely so too; yet the aristocratic taint was there."[19] Ruggles suffers from the aristocratic taint, but one of the reasons we like him so well is that he transcends it, at least to a degree. His resolution to invite the cockney Hobbs to the next ball is truly magnanimous, since it was Hobbs who immediately saw through Ruggles and attempted to expose him: "Sets himself up for a gentleman does he? He ain't no more a gentleman that wot I be."[20] But like a true American democrat, Ruggles forgives Hobbs and decides that he may come to the ball, provided " I can become assured that he has quite freed himself from certain debasing class-ideals of his native country. This to be sure is an extreme case, because the fellow is that type of our serving class to whom equality is intolerable. They must from their centuries of servility look either up or down, and I scarcely know in which attitude they are

more offensive to our American point of view. Still I mean
to be broad. Even Hobbs shall have his chance with us!"[21]

William Dean Howells found Ruggles "a fresh contribution
to the stock of American humor," though he suggested that
here and there Wilson might have taken a hint from Thack-
eray's Charles Yellowplush.[22] This seems unlikely. It is true
that both Ruggles and Yellowplush are satires on snobbery,
but otherwise the resemblance isn't great. On the other hand,
Harry's debt to the traditions of western humor is plain. The
book abounds with such devices as comic similes ("had no
more culture than a jack-rabbit"; "dressed up like a broken
arm"; "quicker than hell could scorch a feather"), anticlimax
(Miss Effie's reply to Ruggles' inquiry as to the antiquity of the
Floud family: "The Flouds . . . were living in Red Gap before
the spur track was ever run out to the canning factory—and I
guess you know what that means!"), grotesque exaggeration
(Cousin Egbert's characterization of Miss Effie as a wildcat
"who'd fight a rattlesnake and give it the first two bites"), and
tall lying (the cow persons, Hank and Buck, convince Ruggles
that he does not need to fear the grizzly bear so much as "an
animal quaintly called the 'high-behind,' which lurks about
camping-places such as ours and is often known to attack man
in its search for tinned milk of which it is inordinately fond.
The spoor of one of these beasts had been detected near our
campfire . . .").

The incongruities between American and British usage
which Wilson pointed up in *Ruggles* delighted H. L. Mencken
as did the character of the butler himself. Addressing Wilson
as "M. le Maitre," he wrote, "I have just finished Ruggles and
hasten to whoop my congratulations across the intervening
Cordilleras. A superb piece of work! 'Bunker Bean' was a very
fine performance, but it seems to me that you have got a much
better comic idea in the new book, and that you work it out
with greater ingenuity and effectiveness. The thing never falls
down an instant. Time and again I thought that I was coming

upon a flabby place, but always it bucked up and went on more vigorously than ever. The thing is a scream from the first page to the last, and there are spots in it that belong to the very highest sort of satire. For example, the scene between Ruggles and the Hon. Geo., in which they discuss the American habit of using "I guess." Again, the various scenes in which Ruggles struggles with the American spirit of American equality. More than once I was reminded of Huck Finn's memorable decision to go to hell. I get my review into the June S.S., out May 15th."[23]

Comparisons between Ruggles and P. G. Wodehouse's Jeeves are inevitable, but if any indebtedness exists it must be in favor of Wilson, for Ruggles arrived in America in December 1914, three years before Jeeves was conceived.[24] Actually, the similarity between these two gentleman's gentlemen isn't great. Jeeves is simply the clever servant of Plautine farce brought up-to-date. Possessed of one of the great minds of our time, he is able to extricate his master from all sorts of scrapes. Ruggles, on the other hand, has only normal intelligence. Though a competent valet, he is not a quick thinker. From his tribulations he emerges victoriously not because he has superior mental equipment, but because underneath his flunky mannerisms, he has the instincts of a decent human being. In times of crisis when he is forced to act instinctively the fine traits of the unspoiled natural man come to the fore. Realizing that Cousin Egbert and Jeff Tuttle have treated him as an equal, he cheerfully shoulders the blame for getting them drunk. Again, the unthinking haymaker with which he responds to Belknap-Jackson's kick shows that his reflexes were sound. He is a deeper character than Jeeves, and the novel in which he appears is so much more thoughtful than anything in the Jeeves-Wooster saga that Herschel Brickell's remark that "P. G. Wodehouse will never see the day when he might be entitled to hold a candle for Harry Leon Wilson to write by"[25] seems entirely just.

One of the most entertaining characters in *Ruggles of Red Gap* is Mrs. Lysander John Pettengill, the owner of Arrowhead ranch. Wilson introduced her into the novel merely as a foil for Ruggles, but she delighted Lorimer so much that he asked the novelist to develop her further. Harry did so in a series of short stories which for the next twenty years were one of the most popular features of the *Post*. Treating of such topical subjects as the arrival of a hobo poet in Red Gap, the attempt to establish a Latin Quarter there, bazaars for the starving Belgians in World War I, and the coming of winter sports to the West, the stories are now dated. What is permanently interesting about them, however, is the character of Ma Pettengill, the owner and operator of Arrowhead ranch, a really original contribution to the gallery of American humorous types—original because she was studied from life and because no other writer had ever looked closely at the originals from whom she was drawn. In his youth in the West, Harry had met several of her kind—resolute but motherly old hoydens who had braved the perils of the deserts and mountains, shot catamounts and rattlesnakes, and borne children on the floors of prairie schooners and in lonely ranch houses. They asked no quarter from life; if their husbands died, they carried on, operating mines, or ranches, or like Poker Alice Tubbs of Deadwood fame, "honest" faro games. Though some of them smoked, swore, and drank whiskey, they were both respectable and respected by men and women in all walks of life. A composite portrait of Titanesses like these, Ma Pettengill owed little to the comical females created by Harry's predecessors—types like Mrs. Partington, the widow Bedott, Samantha Allen, or even Stockton's Mrs. Lecks and Mrs. Aleshine. On working days Ma, an elderly person of immense bulk, wore a wide-brimmed cowboy hat, flannel shirt, khaki riding-breeches, and heavy boots, but because she was on vacation in the Adirondacks, she was sporting a flamboyant blouse and a gray walking skirt, when Ruggles first met her. In spite of the overwhelming blouse, she impressed him favorably; he liked her broad smiling face, keen eyes and rather blobby nose, but what really captivated him was the "uncouth goodwill" that he heard in her "magnificently hoarse voice."[26] In short, for Ruggles and for Wilson's readers alike Ma came to represent the traditional spirit of the old West—its energy, its hospitality, its warmheartedness, its hatred of affectation, and its direct speech.

All of Ma's stories give the effect of oral tales. They are reported by her paying guest, an ardent field-and-stream man, just as she told them to him as they rode horseback over the range, sat drinking whiskey in her office, lounged on the porch of the ranch while she rolled cigarettes, or after a day of trout fishing, relaxed in the parlor before Arrowhead's open fire. A master of the vernacular, Ma could with a few bold strokes set before her listeners a vivid likeness of anyone who interested her. Take for example her description of an old gal gallantly fighting a rear-guard action against time:

". . . She was fifty if she was a day, but very, very blonde; laboratory stuff, of course. You'd of called her a superblonde, I guess. And haggard and wrinkled in the face; but she took good care of that, too—artist's materials.

"You know old Pete—that Indian you see cutting up wood back on the place. Pete took a long look at her and named her the Painted Desert. You always hear say an Indian hasn't got any sense of humor. I don't know; Pete was sure being either a humorist or a poet. . . ."[27] There's a vast amount of Americana in those few lines and even more in these: "I got to tell you about Metta. She's our artist; gives lessons in oil painting and burnt wood and other refinements. People can take six lessons off Metta and go home and burn all the Indian heads on leather sofa pillows that you'd ever want to see. Also she can paint a pink fish and a copper skillet and a watermelon with one slice cut out as good as any one between here and Spokane. She's a perfectly good girl, falling on thirty, refers to herself without a pang as a bachelor girl, and dresses as quiet as even a school-teacher has to in a small town."[28]

But amusing as they are, it was not merely her caricatures that enshrined Ma in the affections of Harry's readers; what won her a place in their hearts comparable to that enjoyed by David Harum, Mr. Dooley, Pudd'nhead Wilson, and Abe Martin was her incidental observations. Certainly she ranks high among our cracker-barrel philosophers. To be sure, her range is narrow, but within it she is as accurate as Annie Oakley. Nor did she choose inconsequential targets. Isn't prohibition quite as important a fact in American history as the conquest of the Philippines? From the first she opposed what she called "the hydrant-headed monster." In preparation for the drought she laid in a large quantity of Scotch and as she and her guest drank from her ample reserve they agreed that "prohibition might be a good thing for the state of Washington," and that they really ought to deny themselves "for the sake of those weaker natures lacking self-control, including Mr. Bryan," whom the lady characterized as "just a water spout."[29] Like other western humorists, Harry is often too diffuse, but some of Ma's remarks are as concise and quotable as Abe Martin's. Expressions like "till folks began to act too familiar in public and call it dancing;" "Lon doesn't know anything about art, but he knows what his wife likes;" and "at twenty-eight a girl's either married or serious," got out of Harry's books into the speech of his readers, who regarded Ma as a homegrown Rochefoucauld.

The success of *Ma Pettengill* and of *Ruggles of Red Gap* placed Wilson in the front rank of American humorists. George Ade thought him better than Mark Twain[30] and Ring Lardner, who was just beginning his career, measured his own efforts against Wilson's and hoped someday to be as good.[31] Howells wrote Harry a note of appreciation:

Kittery Point
Sept. 28, 1918

Dear Mr. Wilson:

We are reading aloud, rather simultaneously, *Somewhere in Red Gap* and *Ruggles of Red Gap,* and I have been amazed and mortified at the blundering account of your people which I gave in my Easy Chair. No Englishman could have misstated the case worse; but years and a failing mind have reduced a once sprightly American to the lowest British level. The books delight me more than ever, and I wish to drop these tears of shame and regret at the author's feet. It was a great pleasure to see you, which I hope I shall have again.

I am not sure but I like *Somewhere in Red Gap* as well as *R. of R. G.*

Yours sincerely,
W. D. Howells[32]

Some months later in "The Easy Chair" Howells said that reading *Somewhere in Red Gap* (a collection of Ma Pettengill stories) made him feel ten or twenty years younger, "like a man of seventy." He was cheered immeasurably by "the gaiety and lightheartedness of characters" like the old Indian "who puts off his massacres on a brother-in-law who never existed; and cousin Egbert, who was in the other Red Gap book, and that fine old ranch-woman Ma Pettengill." It was his hope that Wilson would not "turn serious or psychological and begin reminding me that we are in the midst of a world war and had better all be dead."[33]

In 1918 Harry Leon Wilson was probably the only popular writer able to please both Howells and Mencken, critics who represented opposite poles of American taste. Between these extremes there were thousands of readers who rejoiced in the doings of Bunker Bean, Ruggles, and Ma Pettengill. Even people who, like Louis Untermeyer, claimed they seldom read the *Saturday Evening Post*, liked his work.[34] He was the friend and benefactor of a broad public.

Notes

CHAPTER FOUR

Carmel

1. Marion L. Starkey, "Harry Leon Wilson in California," *Boston Transcript*, Book section, January 11, 1930, p. 1.

2. Monterey, California, June 24, 1913. Ade papers, Purdue University.

3. Letter, HLW to James Stevens, March 17, 1930. Owned by Mr. Stevens.

4. Letter, Henry L. Perry, Historiographer of the Bohemian Club, to the author, February 7, 1958.

5. William Rose Benét, "The Earlier Lewis," *Saturday Review of Literature*, X (January 20, 1934), 421–422.

6. Letter, HLW to Tarkington. TP.

7. Letter, September 9, 1913. Street papers.

8. Myla Jo Closser, "Harry Leon Wilson, An Interview," *Bookman*, LXI (July, 1925), 458–460.

9. Carbon copy of letter, HLW to Frances Wilson, March 4, 1925. WP.

10. Letter, New York, July 10, 1916. WP.

11. John Tebbel, *George Horace Lorimer and the Saturday Evening Post* (Garden City, New York: Doubleday & Co., 1948), p. 120.

12. "A Satire of High Type," *Literary Review*, II (June 3, 1922), p. 699.

13. *Letters of H. L. Mencken*, selected and annotated by Guy J. Forgue (New York: Alfred A. Knopf, 1961), p. 30.

14. Letter, H. G. Wells to Harry Leon Wilson, undated but headed 17 Church Row, Hampstead. WP.

15. Original in WP.

Cartoon in the card room at the Bohemian Club—Swinnerton portrays a remarkably Wilsonian ancestor holding all the cards.

At the Bohemian Club—left to right, George Sterling, Jimmy
Hopper, H. L. W. and Jack London.

16. (Garden City, New York: Doubleday, Page and Company, 1915), p. 78.

17. *Ibid.*, p. 196.

18. *Ibid.*, p. 368.

19. *The Autobiography of Mark Twain*, ed. by Charles Neider (New York: Harper & Brothers, 1958), p. 273.

20. *Ruggles of Red Gap*, p. 157.

21. *Ibid.*, p. 369.

22. "Editor's Easy Chair," *Harper's Monthly*, CXXXVII (June, 1918), 138–141.

23. Letter, April 16, 1916. WP.

24. Jeeves's first appearance was in 1917 in a story called "Extricating Young Gussie." There he merely announced a visitor and vanished until 1919 when he reappeared in *Leave It to Jeeves*. See John Hayward, "P. G. Wodehouse," *The Saturday Book* (1941), p. 383.

25. *Prize Stories of 1949: The O. Henry Awards* (Garden City, New York: Doubleday and Company, 1949), p. xix.

26. *Ruggles of Red Gap*, p. 96.

27. *Somewhere in Red Gap* (Garden City, New York: Doubleday, Page & Company, 1916), p. 282.

28. *Ma Pettengill* (Garden City, New York: Doubleday, Page & Company, 1919), p. 4.

29. *Ibid.*, p. 78.

30. Fred Charters Kelly, *George Ade, Warmhearted Satirist* (Indianapolis: Bobbs-Merrill Co., 1947), p. 250.

31. Donald Elder, *Ring Lardner, A Biography* (Garden City, New York: Doubleday, 1956), pp. 138 and 316.

32. Letter in WP. Permission to quote this letter has been granted by Professor William White Howells of Harvard University for the heirs of the Howells estate. Republication of this material also requires such permission.

33. *Harper's Monthly*, CXXXVIII (January, 1919), 278.

34. Louis Untermeyer wrote HLW that though Mrs. Untermeyer and he did not usually care much for the *Saturday Evening Post*, both of them were delighted with *Ruggles of Red Gap*. Letter, January 31, 1915. WP.

Laughing Philosopher

LIKE MOST SUCCESSFUL NOVELISTS Harry Leon Wilson admired the great practitioners of his art. As a boy he had, as we have seen, delighted in Bret Harte, Dickens, and Mark Twain, and to them he returned again and again. During the years at Bonniebrook in the Ozarks he became enthusiastic about George Meredith, Joseph Conrad, George Moore, and H. G. Wells. His reading, however, was not limited to fiction; in fact after he settled down in Carmel and began to write the farcical, yet trenchant, novels on which his popularity was founded, he became more and more interested in philosophical problems. They fascinated him so much that in 1917 when the success of *Ruggles of Red Gap* made it possible for him to quit writing for a while he took a year off to study the thinkers whose ideas had built the modern world. At the end of his "sabbatical" he wrote Tarkington that he'd "dipped into Kant, Hegel, Schopenhauer, Spinoza, Herbert Spencer, Tyndall, Huxley, Nietzsche, and a dozen others," and that he now knew "everything—the nature of matter, the law of life and the universe, all about what man is, whence he came, where he's to go, and why. It's a wonderful thing to know all this and be sure that I'm now able to solve all questions."[1]

Harry's "sabbatical" was not entirely voluntary. 1917 was a war year, and he may well have thought that his approach did not suit days of conflict. At any rate he published nothing between October 1916 and April 1918. He was not a pacifist, but unlike most of his friends he had little enthusiasm for the great crusade. Toward the whole affair he was able to take a detached attitude, since he was too old for the draft and Ocean Home was five miles outside of Carmel, then an isolated village reached by stage coach from the railroad at Monterey, five miles away. Echoes of the fighting came to him only faintly, for there was no radio nor television in those days. Yet even in the grimmest times people need to laugh, and so there is always work for a comedian. Eventually, Harry found a subject suitable for his talent in the vagaries of the home front. Accordingly, in May 1918 he related in the *Post* how Ma Pettengill had put the ranch on a war basis, demanding that all the cow hands as well as Lou, the Chinese chef, and Boogles, the aged chore boy, spend their Sunday afternoons knitting, though she was the only one on the place who had been able to catch on to casting off. The story then goes on to tell how Ma lost out in a deal over some mules which were wanted by the army.[2]

Harry wrote three other short stories about the war, all of them published in the *Post* in January 1919, and later collected in *Ma Pettengill*. In "Curls" he has Ma satirize the sentimental stories the magazines had been printing about how war improved the character, "stories about how the tough boy, that robs his gray-haired mother of her wash money to play pool with, goes into war's purifying flames and comes out a man, having rescued Marshall Fotch from a shell hole under fire and got the thanks of the French nation and his hometown paper. Now he don't hang round the pool parlour any more, running down fifteen balls from the break, but shuns his low companions, never touches a cue again, marries the mayor's daughter, and becomes the regular Democratic candidate for county recorder" (p. 307). Ma then relates the story of a village good boy who went through the purifying flames and returned to be the town tough.

In "As to Herman Wagner," Harry tries to allay some of the ill feeling which had been aroused by the baiting of German-Americans, most of whom had been loyal to their adopted country during the conflict. Needing men for her ranch, she hired young Herman Wagner, who hadn't been in America long. "The boys heard he was a German alien and acted, at first, like a bunch of hogs with a bear about; but I'd have hired old Hinderburg himself if he'd offered and put him to doing something worth while" (p. 284). After the boys found he couldn't be enraged by "the foulest aspersions on the character of the Kaiser," they began to accept him; that is they treated him as they treated any other tenderfoot. He fancied himself as a hunter, so they told him all about the game that ran wild on the place—the cross-feathered snee, the filo, and the riffle snake. "Also, they had Herman looking for a mated couple of the spinach bug for which the Smithsonian Institution had offered a reward of five hundred dollars, cash." Herman fell for all of this old stuff, the point being that there is more than one kind of German and "Herman was the other kind."

By far the best story Harry wrote about the war was "The Taker-Up," a satire on those women to whom the tragedy chiefly meant a chance to inflate their egos. Mrs. Genevieve May Popper, a Red Gap society leader of mature years, took up the war in such a hearty girlish manner that Ma felt someone ought to take her aside and as a friend and well-wisher, say to her "Now look here old girl, you might get by at that costume ball of the allied nations as Stricken Serbia or Ravaged Belgium, but you better take a well-meant hint and everlastingly do not try to get over as La Belle France. True,

France has had a lot of things done to her . . . and she may show a blemish here and there; but still don't try it unless you wish to start something with a friendly ally—even if it is in your own house. That nation is already pushed to a desperate point, and any little thing may prove too much—even if you are Mrs. Genevieve May Popper" (p. 260).

Mrs. Popper first took up the Red Cross, but she decided that wasn't for her when she found "young chits of no real social standing, but with a pleasing exterior, could get into a Red Cross uniform costing about two-eighty-five and sell objects of luxury at a bazaar twice as fast as a mature woman of sterling character in the same simple garb" (p. 264). Next she recruited a company of girl ambulance drivers, so that she could dash around the corridors of the hotel in Spokane in a uniform costing two hundred and fifty dollars, complete with shiny boots, silver spurs, natty cap, and Sam Browne belt. But she fell out with the adjutant general or something, and left the ambulance service flat. After that she set out to teach housewives how to practice economy in canning; that is she "showed 'em how to make mincemeat out of tomatoes and beets; how to make marmalade out of turnips and orange peel; preserves out of apple peelings and carrots, and guava jelly out of mushmelon rinds or some such thing" (p. 269). Then she took up a French officer she'd met in the city, entertained him in the palatial Popper home, and, Ma hinted, hypnotized him. "He wan't in good shape, anyway. First place he'd been fighting in the air force for three years and had been wounded in five places—including the Balkins. Then he'd been sent over here as an instructor, had fallen out of a plane and that had given him a nice pleasant vacation on crutches" (p. 272). He was scheduled to speak at the county fair where some of Mrs. Popper's preserves were on display, but just as the program started the canned goods began to explode, and the poor Frenchman, who had suffered from shell shock, took off, leaving the crutches behind.

The philosophical reading Harry did during the war was soon reflected in his writing. In September 1918 in "The Porch Wren," a short story in the *Post*, he has Ma give her opinion of metaphysics. "Metaphysics," she said, "is silly-simple—like one, two, three. It consists of subject and object. I only think I'm knitting this here sock. There ain't any sock here and there ain't any me. We're illusions. The sound of that Chink washing dishes out in the kitchen is a mere sensation inside my head. So's the check for eighty dollars I will have to hand him on the first of the month—though the fool bank down in Red Gap will look on it with uneducated eyes and think it's real. Philosophers have dug into these matters and made 'em simple for us. It took thousands of books to do it; but it's done at last. Everything is nothing. Ask any scientist; he'll make it just as clear to you as a mist in a fog."[3] In the same story two scientists debate the age of our planet; one estimating it at fifty-seven million years, the other at four hundred million. Ma thought the earth didn't look anywhere near as old as that. Playing with ideas like these was something new in popular humor in America. Comparable passages in which the fun arises out of the contrast between philosophical or scientific notions on the one hand and common sense on the other are rare in Ward, Nasby, Billings, Nye, or even Mark Twain. Thus Harry's reading added a new dimension to his writing.

Of the philosophers Harry mentioned in his letter to Tarkington, the one who influenced him the most was Herbert Spencer. Because no technical training in metaphysics was required to follow his thought, Harry, like many other self-educated Americans of that generation, men like Hamlin Garland, Jack London, Theodore Dreiser, and H. L. Mencken, were able to read him with interest.[4] Two of Spencer's dogmas which especially impressed Harry were, first the belief that behind all appearances is the Unknowable (an entity Harry equated with the life force), and second the belief that competition is the method through which the Unknowable works. Both of these ideas he embodied in *Life*, a serious free-verse play which he wrote for the Bohemian Club for their celebration in June 1919. Though impressively staged, this production probably disappointed many of the audience, for it contained not the slightest trace of Harry's humor. It is, nevertheless, an interesting statement of Harry's convictions. In the prologue a mysterious figure called the Sower informs the chorus that it was he who aeons ago sowed star dust, shaped the earth, brought the seeds of life into the universe, and in the fullness of time created man. Why he did all this, he does not know; that secret remains the property of inscrutable forces behind him. He knows only that

> From the heaped hand of star dust
> I spilled in the great void,
> I have brought Man.

For Man, he now sows the seed of the Bush of Wanting, whose fruit, once eaten will set Man's feet upon an endless cycle of pain and ecstasy. Following the prologue, three primitive men —Og, Jad and Tull—gather around the Bush. Og, the eldest, preaches contentment and places a taboo on the fruit, but Jad and Tull eat it, discover Woman, and as a result, love and strife enter the world. Quarrelling over Woman brings about the death of Jad at the hands of Tull, but in due course Jad lives again in little Jad, whom Tull cherishes. By this time all of the tribe have eaten the fruit of Wanting and have learned that Desire is life; Contentment, death. As the play ends, the Sower reappears to proclaim that Man's feet are now set on an ever-rising spiral of Wanting which will bring him through sorrow and delight to a splendid destiny.

Life brings out Harry's belief that the race advances only through competition. In 1919 when radicals of various hues began to question the validity of this doctrine and its economic corollary, *laissez faire*, Harry rushed to the defense with several bits of anti-communist propaganda. In May in a *Post* article called "Naughty Boys," he ridiculed "parlour pinks;" in September in the same magazine published *The Gibson Upright*, a farce attempting to demonstrate the impracticability of socialism; and again in the *Post* in November, in *The Wrong Twin*, a seven-part serial, he reaffirmed his faith in the doctrine of free enterprise.

In this amusing, though melodramatic, tale, the Spencerian creed is expounded by Dave Cowan, a tramp printer who has read and traveled widely and who when the linotype machine renders his trade of hand composition obsolete masters the new machine, thus conforming to the Darwinian imperative that life must adapt itself to new conditions. Dave trusts competition, even though it had threatened to slay him: "They can spray the fire of competition with speeches all they like, but they can't put it out. Because why: Well, because this life thing is going on, and competition is the only way it can get on. Call it Nature if you want to. Nature built star dust out of nothing, and built us out of star dust, but she ain't through; she's still building. Old Evolution is still evoluting, and her only tool is competition, the same under the earth, and on the earth, the same out in the sky as in these states."[5] Dave also believes that "we fought our way up to be a fish with lungs, and then we fought on till we got legs, and here we are. And the only way we got here was by competition—some of us always beating the others. Holy rollers like socialists would have us back to one cell and keep us there with equal rewards for all. But she don't work that way. The pot's still a-boiling, and competition is the eternal fire under it . . ." (p. 227).

Dave is footloose, for although he is a widower with small twin sons, Wilbur and Merle, he allows other people to bring them up. The story of their development affords Harry a chance to attack socialism. Wilbur is cared for by his mother's people, lower middle-class folk. Scorning the white-collar ideals of his school-teacher cousin, he succeeds in acquiring a good practical education, learning to repair automobiles, tractors, and other machines. The other twin, alas, is not so lucky. Poor Merle is adopted by the town banker who sends him to college where his head is filled with socialism and other theories at variance with the plain teachings of biology. Consequently, when the country enters World War I, Merle becomes a slacker, founding a little magazine, *The New Dawn*, to oppose the draft and to reinterpret American history *à la* Charles Beard. According to Merle, our Revolutionary War "had marked the triumph of the capitalistic state— the state that made property sovereign. The Revolutionary fathers had first freed themselves from English creditors, then bound down as their own debtors an increasing mass of the American population. The document known as the Constitution of the United States had been cunningly and knowingly contrived to that end, thus thrusting upon us the commercial oligarchy which persisted to this day. It had placed the moneyed classes securely in the saddle, though with fine phrases that seemed to mean not this" (p. 243). Finally, the long-suffering banker and his family grow weary of Merle's foolishness and by cutting off his allowance, force him to give up his magazine and return home. Wilbur, in contrast, like the good citizen he is, goes to war, becomes a hero, and on his return is rewarded with the hand of the banker's daughter.

Harry's defense of the status quo in *The Wrong Twin* and in two or three articles he wrote for the *Post* in 1919 cost him some readers among liberals, several of whom wrote him letters bitterly protesting his opposition to socialism: "You were the whole show in *The Saturday Evening Post*," wrote one of his former admirers resentfully, "and we bought the rest of the junk because it was the only way we could get your weekly installment, and read it aloud to each other. . . . Your present stuff is calculated to save the gentlemen who profit by anarchy hugely. Certainly they should pay and pay big."[6]

In accusing Harry of being a hireling of big business, these

zealots showed no understanding of his character and pur-
poses. Had it occurred to any of them to point out to him that
Proudhon had long ago noted that "competition drives out
competition" or that Prince Kropotkin had showed that co-
operation was as natural as competition, they might have con-
verted him, for Harry was a reasonable man, willing to follow
truth no matter where it led. In any event, it would have been
interesting to see what replies he might have found to the
arguments of Prince Kropotkin. But his socialistic opponents
did not argue; they simply called him names.

Harry ignored most of their letters, but to one of them, because the critic was "nice enough not to ascribe an unworthy
motive to me," he wrote a seven-page reply, insisting that he
published only what he honestly believed, that his view of
competition was grounded on the "teachings of biology and
organic evolution—and its extension, social evolution," and
that in the United States needed changes could be brought
about by evolution rather than by revolution. The people he
wished to castigate, he went on, were those "who smugly and
falsely assume that we have the same government here and
should apply the same remedy of revolution as the Russians,
the people who have profited by our system, who have been
nurtured, educated, well-paid for their work here. . . .

"You must know this class as well as I do. I don't believe
you know them better, for as I tell you, I was one of them for
a good many years. I know their jargon, their cant phrases
and their aimless bitterness. And I was one with them in their
belief that they form the one intellectual aristocracy—that
people who disagree with them are either corrupt or stupid.
Whereas, for seeing the world as it is, for comprehension of
the scheme under which we find ourselves on this earth, for
plain solid thinking, they are not worth a hoot. At least I have
never known one that was. And I have never known one that
has been a hundredth part of the value to the world that John
D. Rockefeller has. . . .

"It isn't a pretty thing, this affair of human life; we must sentimentalize it to make it at all tolerable. But for God's sake don't blame me for its manifold infelicities, and don't blame me if I take a different view from yours, or think that I am necessarily unworthy or an enemy of the proletariat or an upholder of privilege. Start from where we are now and I'll applaud any experiment you want to try. I rejoice in that lovely strike they have just pulled off in Winnipeg. I am watching North Dakota. I am watching England. The wise ones tell me that England will be a labor republic in from three to five years. Probably so. England is compact and boiling. But if it comes there I think it will come without sacrifice of useful parts and foundations already evolved.

"Me? I'm just an interested watcher. I wouldn't for the world interfere with any experiment now under way any-where on earth. But when I see lessons that can be learned, say from Russia, I shall not fail to point them out."[7]

In 1923 Harry and Mrs. Wilson took a five-month cruise to Australia, New Zealand, Java, and southern China, partly for a vacation, partly to gather material for "Adventures in Geog-raphy," a series of articles he published in the *Post* from June 21, to July 19, 1924. The pieces on Australia and New Zea-land attempt to show how governmental interference and union labor were impeding the development of those coun-tries.[8] Of more importance in the light of later developments are the installments on Java and China, both of them over-populated lands. Harry's reading in Spencer had kindled his interest in the Malthusian theory, and one reason he wished to go to the Orient was to see the effects of overpopulation at first hand. His conclusions were gloomy. The Dutch, he as-serted, were trying an experiment in Java; they wanted to find out how many small brown people the island would hold. In the hundred years of their reign the population had increased eightfold and the condition of the people was now so miser-able that the end of Dutch rule could easily be foreseen. The article on China was even more ominous. There Harry found people living close to the border of subsistence and doing it so effectively that he was certain Americans could never compete with them. The Chinese, he prophesied, would in two or three thousand years inherit the earth, since they were the people best able to sustain mind and body under the adverse pressures of overpopulation. His observations, he said, confirmed the dire predictions of Professor E. M. East, the Harvard geneticist, who in his book, *Mankind at the Crossroads*, maintained that within a hundred years the world would be "a seething mass of discontented humanity struggling for mere existence."[9]

One might suppose that a believer in social Darwinism would also be an imperialist, but Harry was not. He felt that imperialism with its numerous bureaucrats and its endless regulations hamstrung business. In Java he visited what he called a "perfectly good" opium factory operated by a Dutch governmental monopoly. This authority, he conceded, made some money, but he was certain that its profits would increase if it were operated in the American tradition of free enterprise, since demand would then be stepped up through the use of snappy advertising slogans like "from the poppy to the pipe," and so on. His point, of course, was that imperialism was wrong both morally and economically, and because of its inefficiency it could not last.

We live in a very different world from Harry Leon Wilson's. To us everything Harry learned from his reading in Spencer and in William Graham Sumner, Spencer's American disciple, seems at least debatable. Faith in progress, in the blessings of competition, and in the importance of the individual has waned while faith in the welfare state and in collectivism has waxed. Today many of us believe that as the population grows, individual freedom will have to shrink, that the time will come when some governmental agency will even tell us whether or not we may have children. Harry's belief in the doctrines of Herbert Spencer was naive, yet before we condemn him for uncritically accepting those doctrines, we should remember that many men with greater educational opportunities than his were quite as uncritical. In 1917 such brilliant minds as Nicholas Murray Butler, Charles William Eliot, Elbert H. Gary, David Jayne Hill, Henry Cabot Lodge, Elihu Root, and Harlan Fiske Stone were still acclaiming social Darwinism.[10]

The doctrines of Spencer seemed to fit that era. In fact Harry's intellectual posture was not very different from H. L. Mencken's with whom he liked to argue the merits of Nietzsche:

Carmel, Calif.
November 21, 1933

Dear Mencken:

Thanks so much for your book. And first, what a lovely book the machine turned out—paper, print, boards.

Reading it was an adventure. Not "vealy" as you suggested. Nor had you perfected that noble corn-husking technique which in later years was to stand you in such good stead. Here you are practically meek. Somewhere I find that dear old wheeze about women being less honest than men and I was startled by "the typical woman." So you must have written back in the perhaps late golden twenties when we overflow with nothing less than the most gorgeous certainties; when a possibility, a perhaps, is considered, and doubtless is at that age, the sign of a mental incompetent.

As to Nietzsche, of course, I see now that Salter never got under his hide; probably afraid to, recalling your scandal about his ecclesiastical ball and chain. And yet, you, too, leave me as Salter did, saying with deeper conviction "poor Nietzsche!" So keen, so fine a brain, condemned to torture from the start. His Apollo-Dionysus thing was a good mental play, but what about Nietzsche himself as a Dionysian? To me he seems under-engined, never functioning happily as most of us D's do. To me, again, he will forever be Nietzsche the Feeler, rather than the Thinker, and all because I find him over-emotioned, as incongruous in his world as the butterfly in hell, the orchid in Pittsburg. Captured, burned at the stake like any heretic or witch, but those same emotions. The telegram to Brandes, to make it flatly literal, should have been signed The Self-crucified.

What a queer, baffling mental outfit, a constant challenge. You will doubtless consider my crude diagnosing as stupid as the average, but at least I haven't called him a neurasthenic nor do I say that an orchestra, beer and a girl would have helped him. (At that, privileged to an evening with the man, I should in my poverty of curative measures most likely have looked for an orchestra, the right Pilsner and a couple of comely cowish maidens; the orches. giving us Beethoven or even something so banal— though always grand to me—as the Tannhauser overture. This, of course, before N. unveiled Wagner's shame—that he was ONLY an artist.)

Is it a gift for cold introspection I miss? And in his tortuous slave-moral windings, immoralist, blonde-beast, superman hocuspocus I am now startled by seeming to detect a lyric kinship between our friend and the Southern hillbilly. Redacteur of an Arkansaw weekly wouldn't he have put out more than one choice bit for your spicy Americana?

Schopenhauer, more robust, played a pleasant game with words (as all philosophers do). Poor N. took the game more seriously. And now I am beset with another preposterous suspicion: that here in our day he would have been a spectacular New Thoughter. (Laugh that off, Old Top!) He would have loved Emerson with a father's love, teaching the kid to walk. Good old "Environment!" What would us wise boys do without the word? From a late reading of Self Reliance, for example, I suspect that R.W.E. with Al Capone's advantages would now be in some good jail for more piquant reasons than mere tax evasion (the foible of a gentleman). At least a noisy IWW and perhaps wearing under a lapel, the Gang's gold medal for discovering that the shotgun as a factor in social dissonances can be sawed off to advantage, giving it a bit of sadly-needed subtlety without at close range impairing its native merits.

Another guess at environment: back in pre-mammal times, epicene days if any such ever were, Nietzsche, as advanced protoplasm, would still have worried himself to death: he'd have detected certain cells conspiring to build a vermiform appendix, or, better, insisting that the v.a. was to become necessary, against conservatives insisting that all cellular energy should be centered on starting Sex. N. would have foreseen and passionately preached that Sex would raise merry hell. Anyway and however, he'd have crazed himself back there. I can see no peace at any time for the over-emotioned organism.

And this same affliction spots the man for me as a possible dupe of the C. S.'s. I'm not sure that Science and H. wouldn't have been a help to the man. And, mark my words, some day, probably while you and I both infest the earth, an Advanced School of New-thoughters will have as their chief text-book a tome composed of Nietzsche pluckings—which we will both buy for the ghastly laugh. The N. T.'s, the craz-

ier ones, suffer as N. did: over-emotioned, and here
and there, of course, despite the trumpery bosh of
their postulates, one does get results by training the
emotions to promote certain cellular, gladular activities—something our friend never learned to do.

So here we are in the zoo, clumsy amateurish
mechanisms, laboriously built by a force I try to think
of as blind in order to avoid anthropomorphism. And
I've never been able to feel concerned over the problem of human association which tore so cruelly at
Nietzsche's entrails. I have a better guess than any
I've come on as to how and why the thing started
but only the mildest interest in its wayside mishaps;
which is why a lot of N's real thinking goes over
me. Marriage, democracy, religion—never do I sweat
about them.

I am still hoping the Antichrist will do more than
attack my creed as a staunch Wesleyan, yet blas-
phemy lost its kick for me ages ago. Admitting that
the Nazarene was a (probably inferior) country car-
penter with certain outstanding social gifts and a
monstrous delusion of grandeur, I can no longer be
intrigued by argument to that effect. I'd sooner tell
a Dry that his tribe never cared a damn about my
drinking excesses. It only wanted to coerce and annoy me (Will to Power!) and it did that same. Cost
me money, too. My poor French bootlegger, Louis,
led to believe for years that a pleasantly gainful
pursuit was assured him for life, finds it suddenly
snatched away by a treacherous government. Result: Louis owes me six hundred plunks borrowed
money. I can't argue about that nor with a Calvinist
sending unelect infants to hell. Once I argued. Aged
about nine I wrote a Sunday-school paper superbly
entitled Poor Judas. To the effect that big-hearted

Judas, learning it had been written that one of his bunch had to betray the Master took the load on himself to save another. I recall it as not so badly argued that Mr. Hoyt, the minister, patted my head and smiled, though even then I detected a certain pained difficulty in that smile, benignant though it had to be.

A word more of this gruelling diatribe, another diagnosis of N. and all of us. Years ago, staying with Jack London, I was moved to talk with a sad-faced woman doing the wash. She (after my question), "Well, sir, my poor husband since early manhood has been a sufferer from pragmatism."

Me: (The word wasn't so common then, and to this day I don't know what it means.) "What is that?"

She: "Near's I can make out it's one of these here kinds of mental rheumatisms that just ties you in a knot and leaves you awful complaining."

Again my apologies. I had to get this off my chest and you were the only fair target.

Truly, Monsieur le Maitre

Me, so superior to N. for his emotion-mania. But why not, having learned midway of my 67th year that the nearest I can come to an emotion now is when, on a golf-green, by raw chance which will seem to my opponent like veritable necromancy (if the poor fish knows such a word,) I sink a long, long, putt?

And I can still argue about Free Will. Having been convinced by patient logicians that there can't be any such, I merely bow the lower to whatever cosmographer devised the illusion of that same. Me in a poker game dealt two tens and four spades. The pot opened. Shall I split the tens and draw to the flush? I'm ready to believe my decision was fixed

back in Cro-Magnon days. Yet the illusion of free
choice is perfect. If I didn't have it would I ever
draw cards, or permit the life force to continue
functioning through this present imposing device:
I now regard that superbly cunning illusion as the
crowning achievement of someone or something. I
confess frankly I couldn't have cosmogonized as
well.[11]

The illusion of free will as he experienced it in games was
one of Harry's favorite topics at the Bohemian Club in San
Francisco, where a cartoon still hanging in the card room
commemorates his eloquence on that subject. The picture,
entitled, "You Can't Beat Your Past," is the work of James
Swinnerton of Little Jimmy fame and shows Harry grimly
playing cards with a gorilla whose features resemble his but
whose hand is much the better.

Harry's theory of the comic was of a piece with his natural-
istic outlook. He often remarked that the sense of humor was
merely the ability to see a person or a situation from two
points of view simultaneously. He told his son that examples
of this sort of perspective were frequent in the writings of
Jean Henri Fabre, the French naturalist, who perceived that
the maggot was not only loathsome but also admirable in that
she treated beggars and kings with true equality. Fabre's *Life
of the Fly* gave Harry a great deal of pleasure. "In a cabin I
had up in the hills," he wrote to a friend, "I one day slapped
at a big shiny fly and sort of squashed him against a window
pane. He wasn't dead, only hurt, and buzzed with his wings.
Almost at once a procession of ants marched out from a crack
and began to butcher the victim. They went first to his wings
and soon had those stilled, several holding his legs while the
wings were worked on. Then half a dozen went to his head
and pulled on it. I'd never known what a long neck a fly has.
After they got him all quiet they began to tear him apart.
Gruesome, especially if you magnified the creatures and their

kill to the size of prehistoric monsters which I artistically did. The wings and legs were severed, and the head, and all carried off into the home larder. Then they began on the carcass. They'd pull out an intestine, three or four at first, then others as it lengthened, like men pulling on a cable. Others digging away at other parts. There were probably thirty of the ants, working with an intelligent co-operation—all except one. Terribly funny. He was a clown ant, getting in every one's way, rushing from one group to another, eager to help, but weak-minded. For the ten minutes I watched he never did a single, useful thing. He'd start to help pull or something, then look up and rush off to another job. Quite probably, though, he considered himself the most important worker there. The others paid no attention to him; when he got in the way they went around him. And in ten minutes the prize had been cut up and lugged off—not a tiny trace left. Fabre would have got more than I did out of it, but I got a lot."[12]

According to Harry, since annihilation is the fate of man, our lives are from the point of view of the individual as absurd as those of flies, ants, or tadpoles. "Existence," he said, "is utterly preposterous," thus anticipating the currently fashionable tenet of the existentialists by over thirty years. But Harry differed from these pessimists in that he believed that from a cosmic point of view everything looks promising: In a newspaper interview he once said, "Here's this earth of ours—a ball of fecund mud thrown up at one corner of the universe. We've come a long way since we crawled out of the slime and we've got a long way still to go. Desire is the force that moves us. Men want to live to be 200 years old and someday, because that is what they want, they will live to be 200. But suppose the human race doesn't get very much farther. Our world may turn out to be an unsuccessful experiment, a bum apple on the tree. There are plenty of others. It's absurd to suppose this is the only one that's inhabited. Interplanetary communication will be one of the next things to come. . . ."[13]

Harry was fond of illustrating the absurdity of the life of the individual by comparing it to a game of cards that we are not supposed to win. In his view heredity, environment, and necessity had stacked the deck against man, yet the silly fellow continued to play, hoping that somehow he'd out-luck his opponents. Once in the person of Ma Pettengill's paying guest he voiced another reason why man keeps on: he's tricked into it. "Life, to me is like a trout stream winding through a canyon. You fish along, getting one here and there, but what keeps you going isn't the fish; it's that you want to see what's around the next bend. If you come to an open space where you can see ahead you lose interest, but as long as a bend hides something you keep on. Of course it's foolish; you know it will be the same old creek, but something goads you. It says maybe you'll find a pool better than all other pools, and bigger fish. You don't believe it with your head, but something else believes it and you can't quit, whether the fish are few or many. That's why we keep going till the dark comes and we suddenly realize we're ten hard miles from home or a good twenty years or some such matter."[14]

Passages as sincere and as thoughtful as this are rare in popular fiction. Though Harry wrote for money he was no mere manufacturer of tosh. His humor rested upon a consistent philosophy, the philosophy of materialism. This, as Santayana long ago pointed out, is a position especially conducive to humor because humor depends upon the ability to contemplate the incongruities of existence with something like the detachment of a scientist. According to Santayana, Democritus, the laughing philosopher, was able to contemplate with an active, joyful, somewhat scornful mind, the greatest incongruity of all—the incongruity between private hopes, wishes and illusions on the one hand and the laws of nature on the other. In an unpretentious way Harry could sometimes do that; he was, let us say, a Carmel Democritus.

Notes

CHAPTER FIVE

The Laughing Philosopher

1. "H. L.: A Writing Man," *Saturday Review of Literature,* XX (August 12, 1939), 10–11.

2. *Ma Pettengill* (Garden City, New York: Doubleday, Page and Company, 1919), p. 3–37.

3. *Ibid.,* pp. 188–189.

4. Richard Hofstadter, *Social Darwinism in American Thought* (New York: George Braziller, Inc., 1959), p. 33.

5. (Garden City, New York and Toronto: Doubleday, Page and Company, 1921), p. 277.

6. Letter from Kansas City, Missouri, March 15, 1919. WP.

7. A carbon copy of this letter dated March 17, 1919 is in WP.

8. "Adventures in Geography," *Saturday Evening Post,* CXCVI (June 28, 1924), pp. 8–9.

9. *Ibid.,* (July 19, 1924), p. 61.

10. *Hofstadter,* p. 50.

11. Carbon copy in WP. The original is in the New York Public Library and not available for verification.

12. Letter, HLW to Zilpha Riley, April 13, 1932. WP.

13. Clipping. *San Francisco Call and Post,* November 26, 1925. WP.

14. "Art for Red Gap's Sake," *Saturday Evening Post,* CXCV (December 16, 1922), 4.

Profit And Delight

THROUGHOUT THE TWENTIES Harry Leon Wilson's serials continued to be a popular feature of the *Saturday Evening Post*. When William Randolph Hearst, in a determined effort to build up the circulation of the *Cosmopolitan*, raided the *Post*'s authors in June 1922, capturing such headliners as Irvin S. Cobb, Peter B. Kyne, and Ring Lardner, one of the first defensive moves Lorimer made was to raise Harry's rates to $2,500 for special articles, $3,000 for short stories, and $30,000 for full-length serials—good prices in those days. "I value your stories more than any others that come to the *Saturday Evening Post* or for that matter any that are now being written," he told Harry.[1] In another letter he said that "the new prices have no reference whatever to the doings of the city slicker who is trying to lure you from your virtuous home and simple surroundings."[2] Later he added that "Sam [Blythe] and you are the only two men through whom he could really give me a jolt."[3] In still another letter he joyfully announced that the dramatic version of *Merton of the Movies* "seems to be hitting them where they live," and added that he hoped Harry was hard at work on some other stories.[4]

Harry's popularity with the readers of the *Saturday Evening Post* was well deserved. Like all successful popular art, his work was functional in the lives of the public for which it was created. For the average provincial middle-class American it performed a variety of services. It made him laugh, it voiced his opinions on current trends, it answered questions he had been putting to his environment, and it reassured him that though his job might be humble, it had as much meaning as the work of those who built the aqueducts and the splendid roads of Rome.

Among the most useful of Harry's achievements are the five comical novels he wrote at Ocean Home between 1912 and 1925: *Bunker Bean, Ruggles of Red Gap, Merton of the Movies, Oh Doctor!* and *Professor How Could You!* As a group they are superior to Harry's earlier work in that they are less sentimental and more clearly focused upon a central character. In each of these five stories this character is an innocent who blunders about amusingly in a booby-trapped world. He is, however, a teachable innocent who, on discovering what he needs to know, achieves a firm footing. Meanwhile, in the course of his adventures, he enlists the sympathy of the reader who often comes to identify with him. As one critic observed, *Bunker Bean* "is the pathetic and childlike soul of America— and indeed of man. . . . An absurd, heartbreaking boy, compounded of 'let's pretend' and of tragic sincerity—you, in a word, and me!"[5] All of Harry's other innocents are, like Bunker Bean, symbols in which his readers could discern something of themselves.

As we have already considered *Bunker Bean* and *Ruggles of Red Gap*, we shall in the present chapter try to show how the three comical novels Harry wrote in the twenties—*Merton of the Movies, Oh Doctor!* and *Professor How Could You!*— functioned in the lives of their readers. Merton Gill, the hero of the first of these, was a pathetic little clerk in a village general store who read fan magazines as avidly as Don Quixote

read romances and who, having set his heart on becoming a
movie star, invested his savings in a correspondence course
in acting, did calisthenics to broaden his shoulders, and even
prayed that God would make him one of the best movie
actors. When he finally got to Hollywood, he nearly starved
before the Montague girl, a young but experienced trooper,
sensed his possibilities as a comedian and got him a part in a
farce which he mistook for a serious drama. His unconsciously
ludicrous performance in this was so successful that he decided to renounce his impossible ambition and become what
God intended him to be—a comedian. Thus, by teaching the
necessity of renouncing impossible ambitions, the fable les-
sened somewhat the sting of failure in the heart of the common man. In addition, it brought him many a hearty laugh
over the naivete of a country youth who could write the
following letter:

Dear Friend Tessie:

Well, Tessie, here I am safe and sound in Hollywood after a long ride on the cars that went through
many strange and interesting cities and different
parts of the country, and I guess by this time you
must have thought I was forgetting my old friends
back in Simsbury; but not so I can assure you, for I
will never forget our long talks together and how you
cheered me up often when the sacrifice and struggle
seemed more than any man could bear. But now I
feel repaid for all that sacrifice and struggle, for I am
here where the pictures are made, and soon I will be
acting different parts in them, though things are quiet
on the lot now with only two companies shooting today; but more companies will be shooting in a few
days more and then will come the great opportunity
for me as soon as I get known, and my different capa-
bilities, and what I can do and everything. . . .

There is some great scenery around this place, including many of the Rocky Mtns, etc. that make it look beautiful, and the city of Los Angeles is bigger than Peoria. I am quite some distance out of the center of town, and I have a nice furnished room about a mile from the Holden studios, where I will be hired after a few more companies get to shooting on the lot. There is an electric iron in the kitchen where one can press their clothes. And my furnished room is in the house of a Los Angeles society woman and her husband who came here from Iowa. Their little house with flowers in front of it is called a bungalow. The husband, Mr. Patterson, had a farm in Iowa, six miles out from Cedar Falls, and he cares little for society; but the wife goes into society all the time, as there is hardly a day just now that some society does not have its picnic, and one day it will be the Kansas Society picnic and the next day it will be the Michigan Society having a picnic, or some other state, and of course the Iowa Society that has the biggest picnic of all, and Mr. Patterson says his wife can go to all these society functions if she wants, but he does not care much for society, and he is thinking of buying a half interest in a good soft-drink place just to pass the time away, as he says after the busy life he has led he needs something to keep him busy, but his wife thinks only of society.

I take my meals out at different places, especially at drug stores. I guess you would be surprised to see these drug stores where you can go in and sit at the soda counter and order your coffee and sandwiches and custard pie and eat them right there in the drug store, but there are other places too, like cafeterias, where you put your dishes on a tray and carry it to your own table. It is all quite different from Simsbury. . . ."[6]

As this letter shows the humor of *Merton of the Movies* arises from the fact that Merton acts on assumptions at odds with the reader's idea of reality. The reassuring implication of the fable is that if poor, simple Merton could land on his feet, the reader, whose grasp of reality was much firmer than Merton's, could muddle through. *Oh Doctor!*, Harry's next novel, was another attempt to bolster the reader's morale in the face of the ills of life. Rufus Billop, the central character, is a twenty-two-year-old hypochondriac who from early childhood had had an abnormal fear of death, even though his father and his uncle as two of America's leading morticians had made a splendid thing of it. Their victory Rufus saw, had been only temporary; in the end death had taken them as well as his mother, leaving him to be brought up by an aunt whose chief concern was the avoidance of microbes. As a tutor for Rufus, she hired a young disciple of Schopenhauer named Cleaver, who had once hoped to become a minister, but who had given up his theological course when simultaneously assailed by acute gastritis and doubts as to the authorship of the Pentateuch. Though the gastritis cleared up, the doubts remained, and Cleaver having decided that art is decadent; civilization, dying; and life, a disease, converts Rufus to this creed. Naturally, the boy is bewildered when Cleaver repudiates it by marrying Rufus's aunt. Spiritually adrift, he goes to live with another aunt in Los Angeles. She is not well-to-do, and Rufus, who stands to inherit the Billop fortune if he lives to be twenty-five, becomes a prey to money lenders. Luckily, his problems, both financial and psychological, vanish when a pretty nurse falls in love with him. She outwits the loan sharks, and Rufus, no longer fearing death, now defies it by operating his motorcycle and his high-powered car at tremendous speeds.

In part *Oh Doctor!* voiced the common man's reply to the sad young men who in the early twenties went about wailing with Scott Fitzgerald that all wars had been fought and all gods were dead. T. S. Eliot may have felt as used up as "The Waste Land" indicates, but many of his and Fitzgerald's readers took up pessimism simply because it was fashionable. The pose seemed as silly to the common man as it did to Harry's friend, Thomas Beer, who in a letter to Harry noted, "There is a good deal of Sadness of Life around just now. The Victrola people are advertising a new plate of 'The End of a Perfect Day' with the sub-title Mrs. Warren G. Harding's Favorite Song; I went to a movie the other day and saw a picture of Jack Dempsey being kind to his mother; the Ziegler Funeral parlours in East 24th Street announce 'natural expressions perfectly maintained' and Henry Ford's life is running in Hearst's International. . . ."[7] Accordingly, Harry's story preaches that life is meant to be lived with gusto, that it is an amusing show to which we are lucky to be admitted on any terms, and that we should "die protesting— die hard."[8]

The hero of Harry's next novel, *Professor How Could You!* is Algernon Copplestone, Ph.D., of the history department of Fairwater College. An appealing little man who wished that he might have lived in the age of discovery and gone exploring, he was tired of the close supervision of his wife, "a big broad thinking woman" interested in politics. When she was elected mayor of Fairwater, he decided he had had enough, and his courage artificially stimulated by several glasses of sherry tendered him by a waggish colleague, he determined to leave home, disguised as a tramp. The informal sabbatical which followed was rich in educational experiences such as aiding a bootlegger evade a group of hijackers, playing the role of Indian chief in a medicine show, doubling for the wild man from Borneo in a carnival, becoming involved in the marital difficulties of an emancipated woman in a trailer camp, and working in a hamburger stand. Eventually realizing that no man can escape his fate, he returned to Fairwater and Mrs. Copplestone, but his travels among strange men and cities had not been in vain, for his wife now understood he could be pushed just so far.

In each of these five comical novels the little man, stumbling about on a slippery terrain achieves, temporarily at least, a safe footing through the aid of some incarnation of the Great Mother, that is of Nature. Thus Bunker Bean is encouraged by the flapper's grandmother, the Demon; Ruggles finds his true niche when Ma Pettengill hits upon the idea of his opening the United States Grill in a vacant business building she happens to own; and Merton becomes a comedian under the direction of the Montague girl, who, as Lee Wilson Dodd saw in 1922, stands for the *Ewig-Weibliche*. She and Merton, said Dodd, are not just comical lovers but an embodiment of the idea of the "eternal mother and the eternal child."[9]

Any suspicion that Dodd was reading too much into the story will be quickly dispelled by a perusal of the scene in which Merton, realizing that he has been tricked through the connivance of Miss Montague, better known as "Flips," nevertheless finds comfort in her arms. "There, there," she says, "your mother's got you now and she's never going to let you go, never going to let you go." Dodd was no hack reviewer but a critic of parts whose academic experience included teaching posts at Sarah Lawrence, Smith, Vassar, Wesleyan, and Yale. At the time of his death in 1933, he had just been appointed to fill the chair vacated by George Pierce Baker at the Yale School of the Drama. The author of the dramatic version of *Bunker Bean*, he believed to the end of his days that Harry Leon Wilson was a greater writer than many of Wilson's numerous readers ever suspected.[10]

But to return to the Great Mother. In *Oh Doctor!* she is, of course, the kindly nurse, but her most satisfying embodiment in all of Wilson's stories is in the person of the Hamburger Queen in *Professor How Could You!* Copplestone first beheld her when, wandering about the midway of a street carnival, he was drawn to her sign, which read "See That Fat Woman, the Hamburger Queen. Boys We Make Them Big. Mustard and Onions Extra." But it was the woman herself who engaged his notice, for as he tells us, "she was beautiful. Not with a classic severity, it is true, but running, rather to a most gracious and appealing amplitude. Technically perhaps her sign did her no gross injustice in the phrase 'that fat woman,' yet one would not, I reflected, unless miserably poor in words, so describe this queenly person. Her lovely rounded arms, revealed to the elbow, were magnificently large, but not fat in the accepted sense. Also they were of a dazzling whiteness, as was her broad low brow—classic, this at least—beneath its smoothed mass of lightish brown hair, and her plump face except where a tinge of shyest pink showed in either full cheek. Nor was this coloring, of a bisque daintiness, artificial, as so often happens in these later days. The woman was natural; she radiated a vast serenity, and the light of her gray warm eyes was the light of a knowing benevolence. She reminded me of something I had often before felt, that beauty lies deeper than line or color. I had watched her serving hungry patrons at the counter she graced, always with unruffled calm as one at the edge of troubling activities but untouched by them."[11]

This incarnation of Pallas Athena let the Professor assist her in feeding the hungry, and though their relationship always remained that of goddess and mortal, the memory of her tolerance and understanding, which Copplestone carried back to Fairwater, remained a solace to him in the midst of other woe:

In one thing I am happy. Mrs. Copplestone has been perturbed by rumors of the outrageous Mrs. Gale; she has brought to me certain reports of my association with New York's favorite emotional actress—that Vera of the stormy eyes—which called for quiet explanation. But no hint of that other—

the woman, vast, serene, witty and all-tolerant—has reached her. One golden memory, untouched untarnished, I may keep for secret rejoicing. This is mine alone; no alien carping shall ever desecrate it. Often I shall think of the woman, something light and with wings.[12]

The golden memory which Copplestone had of the woman, "vast, serene, witty, and all-tolerant," is of a piece with the vision of the Good Mother most of us remember from childhood. Psychoanalysis tells us this mother left us about the time we were weaned, but that a few rare souls—the humorists—take over her role and play it for their own and for our comfort.[13] Thus they cajole us into believing that the Good Mother will some time come back, that the world is not so terrible after all. They are resolutely kind, tolerant, and reassuring, and the common man knows instinctively that the spirit they embody is important for his survival.

Professor How Could You! answers two of the questions which troubled the common man in Harry's day. Harry probably encountered the first of these—what is the chief end of man?—for the first time when as a boy he had to study the Westminster Catechism. The problem is obviously important but the answer which the Catechism gave seemed in the twenties outmoded. Today, the answer at which Professor Copplestone arrived seems scarcely more satisfactory, but at least it is more in keeping with a materialistic and psychologically oriented age. According to the professor, since each man is bound to the rack of himself, "riveted unalterably there," the chief end of man is simply to find the least painful position on that rack.[14] And the professor adds as a corallary that "the only hell that's been proved to date" is our inability to free ourselves from this rack.[15] Copplestone should know; he tried hard to become someone else, but in vain.

The other question which this novel raises is do the humdrum tasks by which most men earn a living contribute anything to civilization. To this Harry returns the Emersonian answer that our work has just as much dignity as the work of the men who built the Parthenon or the Acropolis. Thus as Copplestone and Sooner Jackson speed across the plains of Iowa in their jalopy in the early dawn, the professor reflects on the works and days of the farmer:

> From time to time we passed farmsteads where a single tall tower, stark with a Greek simplicity, loomed in the growing light. My companion said that these were silos, and I was content with hearing the musical name. Though doubtless they serve a utilitarian purpose I have never learned what this may be, nor shall I ever wish to. It seemed to me that these daringly chaste structures had been named by a singer and might well have been erected for their beauty alone.
>
> As dawn grew we observed farm laborers come cheerily forth to their tasks, and saw stout horses, arrayed in harness, being led from capacious barns. The world had roused itself for another day of agricultural endeavor, and I suddenly realized that it must have been like this, on other mornings through all time. At the beginning of recorded history man was doing just this; he must have done it before we had the printed word, and would still be doing it with every recurring daybreak for many years to come. It was at this very moment I caught the full thought that history had indeed been continuous and is by no means at an end or dependent for its life on printed books. In short—and the sense of it was so vivid as to startle—history lay all about me at this moment; history as genuine as had been the petty-state feuds that destroyed the glory of ancient Greece.[16]

Harry's public responded to his stories with the same

warmth with which they had responded to "The Man from Home" in the theatre. They found them both entertaining and relevant to their needs and problems. As popular art, his stories were excluded from what Santayana called "the genteel tradition," or what Oscar Handlin terms "official culture,"[17] that is the fiction, art, music, and architecture which were prized by the real or would-be aristocracy mainly as status symbols. The common man found most of this official culture dull, flat, impractical, and artificial. Curiously enough, in the twenties, some of the *avant-garde* decided that the common man was right. Repelled by the sterility of official culture, they took up popular culture enthusiastically. Gilbert Seldes, the historian of this trend, wrote an entire book praising such examples of the lively arts as the films of Charlie Chaplin, New Orleans jazz, Krazy Kat, and *Archie and Mehitabel*.[18] Though Seldes' book ignored Harry, probably because of his connection with the *Saturday Evening Post*, some intellectuals enjoyed certain of Harry's stories greatly. In 1935 Gertrude Stein said *Merton of the Movies* was "the best book about twentieth-century American youth that has yet been done. I always give it to everyone to read who reads English and always have done ever since I first read it when it was first done." When she visited Carmel in that year Harry was the only celebrity there she wanted to meet. For that purpose she took the trouble to drive out to Ocean Home, where she found him "just like the kind of man who should have written the best American story about a young American man."[19] They passed a pleasant afternoon together. When she first knocked at his door, Harry who had never read any of her books, mistook her, he told his son, for "the lawful wife of an Iowa farmer," but he immediately "fell hard" for her genuineness and straightforward simplicity.[20]

Another intellectual who esteemed Wilson was Robert Littell, who thought that if the passage in *Merton* in which the movie director decides to change the title of *Robinson Crusoe*

"Ruggles of Red Gap" with Charles Laughton (in derby hat), Zasu Pitts (left), Charlie Ruggles and Mary Boland.

Thurston Hall, Edward Brophy, Eve Arden and Edward
Everett Horton as they appeared in "Oh, Doctor."

to *Island Love* and to introduce a steam yacht into the story were dug up thousands of years from now in some American Pompeii, "an archeological posterity would be better able to reconstruct our movies, and with them much of our civilization, than from any other passage book, record, plot, or picture that I know of."[21] Still another intellectual who was a Wilson enthusiast was Professor William Lyon Phelps of Yale, who praised Harry as "a creative and purely American artist whom we can read with delight and whose subtle art is so unpretentious that many fail to see it at all."[22]

But the value of Harry Leon Wilson's work can not be fairly gauged by the enthusiasm or vagaries of a few undoubted highbrows. It must be justified if at all by what it did for the public for which it was written, a public which after all was an important section of the American electorate. To these good people Harry Leon Wilson's stories brought laughter and reassurance. Wilson was, as Thomas Beer said, "the tall ringmaster of a sincere little circus in a real field."[23] He knew that his little circus could not do for his patrons what official culture is supposed to do for the favored few, but he was confident that under his tent the common man could find both profit and delight. That for Wilson justified the whole process.

Notes

CHAPTER SIX

Profit and Delight

1. Letter, George Horace Lorimer to HLW, August 2, 1922, HSP.

2. October 6, 1922. HSP.

3. June 22, 1922. HSP.

4. March 20, 1922. HSP.

5. "A Satire of a High Type," *Literary Review*, II (June 3, 1922), 699.

6. (Garden City, N. Y.: Doubleday, Page & Company, 1922), pp. 62–64.

7. January 17, 1923. WP.

8. (New York: Cosmopolitan Book Corporation, 1925), p. 244.

9. *Literary Review*, *II* (June 3, 1922), 699.

10. *Loc. cit.:* "Mr. Wilson, it is true, is not exactly an obscure or neglected writer; but he is a much *greater* writer than his appreciative public has yet been led to acknowledge and believe . . ."

11. *Professor How Could You!* (New York: Cosmopolitan Book Corporation, 1924), p. 192.

12. *Ibid.*, pp. 339–340.

13. Martin Grotjahn, *Beyond Laughter* (New York: McGraw-Hill Book Company, Inc., 1957), pp. 55–56.

14. *Professor How Could You!*, p. 331.

15. *Ibid.*, p. 329.

16. *Ibid.*, pp. 118–119.

17. "Comments on Mass and Popular Culture," *Daedalus* (Spring, 1960), p. 326.

18. *The Seven Lively Arts* (New York and London: Harper & Brothers, 1924).

19. *Everybody's Autobiography* (New York: Random House, 1937), p. 288.

20. Letter, HLW to Leon Wilson, Beverly Wilshire, Hollywood, April 10, 1935. WP.

21. "A Satire on the Movies," *New Republic*, XXX (May 24, 1922), 382.

22. "As I Like It," *Scribner's Magazine*, LXXXVII (January, 1930), 103–104.

23. "Harry Leon Wilson, the Man from Home," *New York Herald Tribune Books*, June 16, 1935, p. 1.

A Writing Man

HARRY LEON WILSON ALWAYS HOPED that some day he would be able to write a "serious" novel. Like his hero, Merton Gill, he wanted to give the public "something better and finer" than the farcical stories that had made his name a household word throughout the midlands. Once he confessed to Rose O'Neill that he continued to do "the comic stunt" because he was sure he could, at least after a fashion, get away with it, and that he saw himself as a bird that always after a short flight returned to the same perch. Some day perhaps he would be able to soar.[1] *Cousin Jane*, which began in the *Post* for September 19, 1925, was evidently an attempt to leave the perch, but halfway through the book Harry flew back to it once more. This was a pity, because, as Malcolm Cowley noted, the first part of the story was good enough to show he could become "Howells's successor or better" if he wished to give up genial satire for the observation of human nature in the round.[2]

The story traces the education of Jane Starbird, whom we first meet when as an orphan of ten she comes from a fashionable boarding school in San Francisco to live with her un-

119

married and impoverished cousins, the Tedmans—Sarah, aged
twenty-six; Marcey, forty-nine; and Wiley, fifty—in the old
decaying, jig-sawed family mansion just outside of the near-
ghost town of Union Hill, California. Since Sarah is too flighty
to teach her, and Wiley is a bedridden paralytic, Jane's education devolves upon Marcey, whose gentlemanly training in
Europe had unfitted him for life in America. "Education," he
tells Jane, "is only to increase your capacity for pleasure, and
that means to get all the pleasure out of the station to which
God has called you." Since he is uncertain just what God has
in mind for Jane, he decides to follow Rousseau and teach her
only what she wants to learn. To his great relief, she assures
him that her knowledge of fractions and grammar is already
adequate, and so they agree to read together about King
Arthur, Drake, Cortez, Franklin of the Arctic, Marie Antoi-
nette, Napoleon, and Queen Elizabeth.

When Jane is twelve, Cousin Sarah runs away from the old
house and its red plush furniture, marble mantel pieces, what-
nots, chromos, and old clocks. One can't blame Sarah greatly,
for she is looking for a mate and there are no eligible suitors
in Union Hill, but her desertion places a heavy responsibility
upon Jane, who has to learn to manage this California house
of Usher.

Jane does become a good manager, so busy that she scarcely
notices the passage of time, until suddenly on discovering that
she is thirty-two and facing spinsterhood, she tries to establish herself in the city. But she soon returns home to take
care of little Sarah, Sarah's daughter, who has come as Jane
did years before, to live in the old mansion. What Jane has
learned is that there is no such thing as freedom of the will;
one does not do what one wants to, but what one has to.
When she grasps this truth Jane's education is complete.

The book as a whole is disappointing, for though it contains
many good things—the Dickens-like Tedmans, the descrip-
tions of the old Victorian house, and Jane's childhood world

of make-believe—the truth is that as Jane gets older she gets tiresome. Artlessness in a child of ten is often engaging, but wide-eyed wonder at railroad trains, beauty shops, hotels, and department stores doesn't become a woman of thirty-two who is supposed to have explored the world of books with the travelled and well-read Cousin Marcey.

Cousin Jane was only a mild disappointment to Harry; in the remaining fourteen years of his life he had to confront many more serious adversities. A sad turning point in his affairs was the failure of his marriage to Helen Cooke. Their troubles seem almost to have been foreordained by the great discrepancy in their ages and by Harry's belief that because he was old enough to be her father he could completely dominate her. When he learned that she was a woman with a mind of her own, a woman who considered her ideas on family finances worthy of respect, the shock was great. "Friction in the home life," he wrote sardonically in one of his short stories, "may be avoided by one of the parties giving in to the other and letting the wife say how the money shall be spent."[3] Moreover, he was almost pathologically jealous of her. Vivacious, spirited, and charming, she, like most of her friends in Carmel, delighted in taking part in amateur theatricals. When in "Pomander Walk," one of the plays in which she had the lead, a neighbor kissed her with what Harry considered undue enthusiasm, he challenged the fellow to a fight. The thespian, aged forty-five and ten years Harry's junior, accepted the challenge, and at dawn on the appointed day the two men and their seconds met in a sheltered glen on the coast a few miles from Carmel. There, after agreeing to abide by the old English rules that a knockdown constitutes a round and that three minutes shall be allowed between rounds, the duelists stripped to the waist. Then standing chest to chest they pummelled one another with fists encased in light riding gloves. At the end of five bruising rounds the younger man was declared the winner, though Harry disputed the decision.[4]

Of course, the whole affair greatly embarrassed Harry's family and friends. Tarkington, ever loyal to him, tried to pass it off as a joke: "I suppose you saw how the old fool fit a younger one at Monterey last spring," he wrote to George Ade. "He wrote me the truth of how it came about, but his account of the actual disturbance I take to be a lie; though I don't doubt he believes it. He says he *virtually* whipped the other bird, but somehow I got the impression of Charlie Case telling of one of his father's triumphs in such affairs. You remember how 'father' would get his nose between the other fellow's teeth, etc."[5]

Unlike Tarkington, Helen was unable to take all of Harry's vagaries lightly. By February 1926 their differences had become so frequent and sharp that a separation seemed the only solution. Accordingly, they agreed that Harry should establish his own headquarters in Portland, Oregon, where their son was to be put in boarding school, that Helen should stay on in Ocean Home, and that their daughter should be sent to a girls' school in San Francisco.

Why Harry chose to live in Portland is uncertain; he knew no one there. Perhaps he believed that by shifting from Carmel to an entirely different environment he might find inspiration to do the serious novel he still hoped to do. Portland, however, wasn't very stimulating; in fact, to judge from "The Green Land," an article on the Northwest which he published in the *Post* in May 1927, he found "the spinster city," as he called it, somewhat stuffy.[6] It was, he asserted, "a town that has never wildcatted, where at most late suppers cake and lemonade are usually served, though if the party happens to be a fast one, grape juice may be added to the lemonade." Still he remained there approximately three and a half years, living first in the Sovereign Hotel, later in an apartment. During this period, the only writing he published was the article just mentioned and *Lone Tree* (1929), a full-length serial.

Though this novel is not the masterpiece with which Harry

dreamed of closing his career, it is a book of which he had no need to be ashamed. "If *Lone Tree* is not a good novel, I am unable to recognize one," said William Lyon Phelps in 1942.[7] Its central character, Old Ben Carcross, is a salute to the old-fashioned individualistic type of westerner Harry admired. Ben, champion of the durable satisfactions of life, is a Will Rogers-sort of cattleman who, after struggling for years to make a living on his ranch, becomes rich when oil is struck on the least fertile part of it. His wife, unable to stand prosperity, immediately sets out for Paris, taking her father, her brother, and her two sisters along and leaving Ben to look after the ranch. When the story opens, Ben is in New York awaiting their return. Stricken with appendicitis, he very nearly dies, but is well on his way to recovery by the time Mrs. Carcross reaches his bedside. As soon as she knows that he is out of danger, she and her party, now augmented by the addition of a French modiste and an interior decorator, leave for their home town in the state of Washington, where she is eager to get settled in their new town house. Ben resolves not to join her there but to set up a rival camp at his ranch. Accordingly, he follows a few days later with his own party, consisting of an aviator and a professor—both of whom had been his fellow patients in the hospital—a four-month-old foundling he plans to adopt, and two nurses for the baby. (He had never had any children of his own.) After several clashes between the two groups, old Ben finds himself back in the hospital once more, probably facing death, but sure he isn't "licked yet."

The story is meant to illustrate the superiority of a life close to the soil to one devoted to conspicuous consumption. Ben hopes that the little boy he has adopted "will never get big money on his mind. Have him find some work he likes—that cattle business ain't so bad—and he'll be happy at it no matter if it only makes him three meals a day and one cheap suit of clothes a year. That's the way to start a boy; give him some-

thing he likes to do and to hell with the big money."⁸ Big
money, to Ben, is merely a matter of luck, and it's a question
whether it's good luck or bad, for sudden wealth, he says, "is
a lot of loco weed, and some folks eat it and go hay-wire."⁹

Lone Tree ended in the *Post* on August 24, 1929. Two
months later sudden wealth had ceased to be a problem for
many of Harry's readers; perhaps the story with its emphasis
on plain living helped to reconcile them to the stringencies
of the depression.

Most of the reviews of *Lone Tree* were favorable,¹⁰ but
Harry finished the book with a feeling of disappointment. At
sixty-two and conscious of waning creative power, he feared
he had been merely repeating himself. In this depressed state
he was grateful for the following note from James Stevens,
the young Seattle writer whose contributions to the *American
Mercury* had impressed him:

"Yesterday we finished Lone Tree, with lamentations over
quitting the company of old Ben. I think you were quite un-
just to him when you wrote of the book as a rehash of all you
had ever done. There is familiar material in it, true enough,
but that is an essential fact in the work of all big writers. You
read Hamlet and you get the material used by Shakespeare,
and the color, philosophical content, the method, the move-
ment, the scenery—everything that is familiar in his other
work. You know David Copperfield and you know the world
of Dickens. You know Huckleberry Finn and you know where
Mark Twain lived. The stuff of life in Lord Jim and The Res-
cue is the same in both books. And that's the answer. The big
writer does not stop with telling stories and describing events
and people out of his memory, for such writing is only a sort
of sublimated gossip; his creative imagination makes a world,
and it remains the same in all his work. The new characters
he brings into this world are his real creations, and by their
verity and charm each book must be judged. So I give old
Ben a hail and halleluiah as a new person and one of the most

delightful gents ever brought to life. He's a greater character than Cousin Egbert, for example, because life runs deeper in him. I also enjoyed all the other people immensely. And you've worked out some of your finest writing in this book. You've made Western American speech into a language."[11]

Harry had met Stevens, the author of the Paul Bunyan stories, several months before, at a Press Club dinner arranged in Stevens' honor by Stewart Holbrook, then on the staff of the *Daily Oregonian*. The two novelists became good friends and Stevens, who still cherishes "golden memories" of Harry's stories as he and Mrs. Stevens read them to each other in the early days of their marriage, was grateful for his interest.[12] Stevens also recalls meeting Wilson's son, then twelve, at Harry's apartment in the Sovereign Hotel and that the relationship between father and son impressed him as being "something good and fine."

The Seattle author was only one of several young writers in whom Harry took a paternal interest. One of his hobbies was watching the magazines for the work of promising beginners. When he found a story or an article that especially pleased him, he would write to the editor congratulating him on discovering a new talent. Sometimes the editor would pass this praise along to the neophyte. In this way Harry came to know Hugh Wiley, George Milburn, and Thomas Beer.[13]

In January 1928 Helen obtained a divorce and with it the right to live on in Ocean Home, though Harry kept the title to the property. When this arrangement proved too expensive for her, she moved out; and in the summer of 1929 Harry, glad to leave Portland, returned to what he considered "the most attractive spot in California."[14] He loved the quiet and the seclusion of his large redwood house. "It has always been necessary to me that I be detached from crowds; that's why I live in the country by myself," he told a friend. "Here I can get far enough from the world to reduce it to the size of an orange—with the consequent reduction of its troubled people, including myself. And so nothing has ever quite overwhelmed me."[15]

After his return to Ocean Home, Harry went through a fallow period, and it was almost two years before his next serial, *Two Black Sheep*, appeared. Though Lorimer paid him $60,000 for this one,[16] it clearly shows a decline in Harry's powers. The story is simply a warming over of ingredients Harry had used many times before. The background, as in *Merton*, is the movies; the hero, as in *Ruggles*, is a foreigner who succeeds in becoming an American citizen, the chief difference being that this time he is French. Missing from the story are the topical comments which helped to enliven Harry's work in the twenties. No one reading *Two Black Sheep* would suspect that the country was then passing through a major economic crisis. In the depression era Harry had evidently lost touch with his public.

Aware that he had been repeating himself, but unable to quit writing because of financial obligations, Harry at the age of sixty-five deliberately set out to find new material. He reasoned that he must discover his subjects among the interests of a newer generation than that which had hailed *Ruggles of Red Gap*. Accordingly, he went out of his way to make friends with those he considered average young people—nurses, secretaries, and young business men—who ranged in age from the late twenties through the early forties. From time to time he entertained some of them at Ocean Home in order to listen to their opinions and their slang. Most of their talk bored him horribly; it was, he was certain, worse than the radio, which he considered an abomination; but he knew that boredom was the price a vernacular writer must pay for his material. He was willing to pay it; where his work was concerned, he boggled at no sacrifice; he even joined the Elks at Monterey. The sad result of his search for material was an automobile accident which virtually put an end to his career as a writer.

On the evening of June 10, 1932, a nurse, aged twenty-six, whom he was entertaining at dinner, told him that he had taken too many cocktails to drive her home safely. His retort that for sixteen years in varying stages of inebriety he had driven his car without nicking a fender proving ineffective, he gallantly relinquished the driver's seat. This "skilled driver," as Harry called her in a letter to H. L. Mencken describing the mishap,[17] put on the brake at seventy-five miles an hour on a slippery road. The big sedan struck an unyielding bank, skidded fifty feet, and then overturned in a ditch, seriously injuring the driver. At first Harry himself seemed to have escaped with only a deep gash over the right eye and minor bruises, but after coming home from the hospital where he had spent only a day or so, he began to notice lapses of memory. On re-examining him, his physician found his blood pressure so high that he prohibited all alcohol and ordered nightly footbaths.

Since Harry wanted to live, he stuck to this regimen conscientiously. Nearly a year later, he wrote to Tarkington:

"If you want to get a line on your own work, just let a big burly coward of a Cadillac or something as good, swipe you across the bean when you're not looking, as I did. Then you can pick up something of your own, like as if it was by someone you'd never heard of—perfectly new to you. You'd think you'd recall at least the topography of the thing—'how it was coming out' but positively not. A novel experience, What? Result: I've lately read four of my long things with a perfectly legitimate keen enjoyment, becoming a talkative Wilson fan; I really didn't know I was so darned good, at least in spots. And here yesterday I caught myself saying a girl brushed back a lock of her red hair while forty times before I had talked about her sable mane, meaning her black hair. Then giving her red on one page. Gosh! Also I've come on spots where I skipped as naturally as if I'd been reading some one less gifted. Had to remind myself of the facts—one doesn't skip, reading one's own stuff.

"Haven't written a line—not having had an idea for a year. But now I find myself taking notes, putting down sentences, phrases, so probably the gears are beginning to mesh some more.

"The Post thing of yours seems to argue that if you can write again, so can I. If Lorimer has a couple more to print they'll sure have me in action. Maybe I'll be even better! I mean than me—not you.

"And I haven't had a drink for a year. That slap sort of incited my blood pressure and two M.D.'s close-herding me, struck out all alcohol, after I'd been imbibing fluently for forty-five years. Funny, but I let the hard liquor go with never a yearning. I handle it, serve it, almost every day, make cocktails and such, and probably will never again want even a sip. But I do miss the wine. I'd just acquired the tail end of a famous old restaurant in S.F. and I often go into the basement to stand wistful in the presence of a couple of hundred quarts of authentic Burgundy, Chablis, Moselle and so on, but all I can do is give it away to people so unappreciative I know they'd rather have the current Scotch or even gin with a bar sinister. And I'm not even let to have coffee. But once a week I debauch myself with the real stuff. Drink two cups and am inebriated, same as by four stiff high-balls, joyous, approachable, ready to grant any favor. So far the M.D.'s haven't found me out. But that's enough about me.

"Here's something I found in my desk just now—anecdote by Bob Davis, I suppose from his Munsey days. In the mail one morning, neatly typed, he finds The Luck of Roaring Camp. In returning it he courteously explains, 'I solemnly promised Bret Harte on his death bed never to take one of his stories except from him.' Back comes the answer—retort—on a postcard, 'You was a damned fool to make any such promise!' I've been laughing a lot at that. A tinge of bitterness there.

"I suppose it's as foolish of me as ever to talk about your coming out here. All the same I still say it would be the grandest thing you ever did, with your wheels turning the same as ever. And you could fly out in no time. My home here is a spot of real beauty, but think of the new stuff you'd see in between, and the new writing stuff you'd take back with you. All right—I know your excuses.

"Anyway, give me some up-to-date gossip.

Yours,
H.L.W.

P.S. Over by all means.

"Some one sent me *The Gibson Upright* to autograph. I told 'em you didn't write a word of it; I wrote it all. You didn't do a thing but dictate it. But I read it to see what you did. And I remembered Miflin was kind o' like Lincoln Steffens. Which reminded me. Link and his wife now reside in Carmel. His wife—Ella Winter (and try to give me a better name for his wife) has just written a book on Russia, telling the comradely truth about it, I believe.

"Anyway there's a fool nut-kid in Carmel that has a dept. in the weekly Pine Cone and his top-line last week was, 'What this town needs is a new Lincoln Steffens.' I'll bet I was the only one in town who knew how funny that was.

"I sent F.P.A. a good nifty not long ago. Don't know if he used it. Referring to that lousy columnist Walter Winchell, I said he at least has a keen sense of Rumor. Only thing I've written."[18]

One of the most satisfying aspects of Harry's career was his friendship with Tarkington, a relationship which lasted over thirty-five years. The two writers saw each other for the last time in October 1919 when Harry, after a summer of playwrighting with Tarkington in Kennebunkport, left for Carmel. Thereafter, a year would sometimes go by without an exchange of letters, but these breaks, so Tarkington told Adelaide Neall, changed nothing; each knew he could count on the other. Tarkington admired Wilson's humor, and he was convinced that comedies like *Ma Pettengill, Ruggles,* and *Bunker Bean* were harder to do and took more talent than the "searchingly realistic explorations into toughness" or the "profoundly formless aphrodisiacs for the adolescent minds of the physically adult" which critics in the twenties acclaimed.[19]

Harry in turn believed that Tarkington could describe average Americans better than either Sherwood Anderson or Eugene O'Neill whose vogue he attributed to an interest in "exotic or decadent personalities."[20] A performance of O'Neill's *Ah Wilderness!* which he saw in San Francisco in 1934 confirmed this judgment. Having read in certain reviews that "O'Neill had gone Booth Tarkington," he went to see the play, but found that he couldn't watch it out. "When the grim ones determine to be comic the result *must* be distressing," he wrote Tarkington. "If you haven't seen this play, don't! If you have seen it you can bear me out that it's terrible!

"At the end of Act I, I pushed out to the lobby for a smoke —During that in one of those brilliant lilts I'm still capable of, it came to me that I didn't have to go back—especially if I went outside—pretending just for to stroll—and sneaked up the street. And by gosh I pulled it off, reaching here safely. Comic maid, comic old maid, comic souse, comic adolescent— comic small boy with falsetto giggle—everything but a taut rope to trip 'em up.

"And not the least of my distress [was] caused by hoarse, hearty laughers all about—people who'd find April fool jokes— bricks under hat-to-be-kicked too subtle.

"Will Rogers plays Cohan's part here and I expected little from him—but was surprised and think him good. Don't see how any actor could do more with his material. For no reason I could spot, kept thinking of Dave Warfield. Anyway if you've seen the thing, let me know if it's so bad or if I'm plain senile. . . .

"Anyway, you have grounds for a libel suit–against (for one) the New Yorker. And one or the other of you owes me about 6 dollars because tomorrow night I know I'll have to go back after act 1 to see if the rest of it can possibly be as sad–(what is sadder than some one trying to be funny who has no right to?)"[21]

After the automobile accident Harry became more and more loath to leave Ocean Home. According to his friend, Samuel Blythe, the author of many political articles in the *Post*, he seemed to be suffering from a mild form of agoraphobia or dread of crowds.[22] In February 1934 Blythe, thinking a change of scene might do Harry good, persuaded him to attend a conference of *Post* writers at Palm Springs. While there, Harry spent most of his time in his room playing solitaire, or whenever he could find an opponent, dominoes.[23]

At this conference, Lorimer, hoping to get Harry back into production again, suggested that he try writing a serial ridiculing young intellectuals of inherited wealth who had joined the Communists. The theme really didn't interest Harry, who thought a story based on Doc Townsend or Huey Long might be a better bet, but he decided not to attempt either of these subjects because he knew little about congressmen— what they eat, what they wear, and so on.[24]

Concluding that Lorimer's suggestion was after all the best, he began to collect materials, reading among other things accounts of John Reed, but when he finally began to write the story in 1935, he found it difficult to compose. The trouble, of course, was that his material was thin. He had done little first-hand research, he had never seen a rich red, and he was out of touch with the radical movements of the thirties. But Harry believed his trouble was physical, and so he bought a five hundred dollar dictaphone into which he talked the story.

The result was a flimsy book, so far below the standards of the *Post* that Lorimer was forced to turn it down.

The rejection, the first he had received since 1912, was a hard blow to Harry's pride, but he took it with characteristic stoicism. He analyzed the manuscript, found that it was even worse than Lorimer had said, and decided that its weaknesses were due in about equal measure to his having dictated it and to the idea's not having been his own in the first place. Then, like the old professional he was, he put it away in the hope that someday he might be able to revise it acceptably.

Nothing Harry ever wrote was completely bad. *When in the Course*—as the rejected story came to be called—was after all a publishable book. After Harry's death, several persons who had helped him with the manuscript in various ways—typing, suggestions, research—demanded payment. To satisfy their claims his children permitted the book to be brought out in 1940, though they regretted the necessity of letting it appear under Harry's name, as there was little of him in it.

After the automobile accident Harry's memory was not dependable, but his mind was still good and he would not allow himself to believe that he could no longer write. Though he kept trying, it was nearly two years before he was able to publish even a short story in the *Post*. Then in May 1934, to the great joy of his faithful fans, he was back with another Ma Pettengill tale. By the end of the year he was able to complete two more of these, but he had at last reached the bottom of the barrel. His final contribution was "The Prince Orlando," in the issue of January 12, 1935.

As his stories ceased to appear in the *Post* and his following dwindled, Harry was in danger of being forgotten; but the Paramount production of *Ruggles of Red Gap* (1935), starring Charles Laughton, kept his name before the public a while longer. When this movie promised to be an even greater hit than the silent one of 1922 in which Edward Everett Horton had had the lead, MGM invited Harry to come to Hollywood for ten weeks at a salary of $1,250 a week to help film *Ma Pettengill*.[25] Harry hated to leave Ocean Home, but he badly needed money and so he accepted their offer. He soon regretted doing so, for the movies intended to involve Ma with some Chicago gangsters and make her over into a figure of slapstick. Harry couldn't take that, and at the end of three weeks he begged off and came home. The Pettengill film was never made.

Harry was completely out of sympathy with the mass audience of the thirties. Though the Laughton version of *Ruggles* was a memorable hit, he could not sit through it. He admitted that it made the audience laugh, but their laughter, he told Julian Street, was "the yelling idiot laughter that comes from just back of the chin. Easy to determine they had never read the book, nor any other book. Even my Gettysburg address was clumsily forced in—one of the best things I ever wrote. I can believe that people who never read the book may find it a tolerable show, but the book's undoubted readers invariably call it awful."[26] He went on to tell Street that he comforted the MGM people with the thought that "while the Address might be my best bit, still I had once dashed off another morsel they might have Ma Pettengill recite in the course of their picture drama, a thing long widely known, at least outside of Hollywood, as the Lord's Prayer. And if you think they are not taking that suggestion seriously, you don't know your picture people."

Perhaps Harry's peevishness at the moving picture people for bringing in the Gettysburg Address stemmed from his receiving only $10,000, less an agent's fee, for the talking picture rights, whereas he believed Paramount made over a million and a half dollars from the film. At any rate the novel provided a warrant for the scene by making Ruggles an eager elocutionist, who readily consented to read choice bits from the English Lake Poets to the Onwards and Upwards Club, wanted to play Hamlet in Red Gap's little theater, and achieved a local triumph for his rendition of the Declaration of Independence at the Chamber of Commerce's Fourth of July Celebration. In contrast to Harry, most of the critics thought Laughton's reading of the Address one of the movie's most effective scenes.

In spite of Harry's disapproval of the Paramount production of *Ruggles*, the small royalty he got from the movie came like heaven's own grace to him. By 1936 he needed money badly. Where had his savings gone? When his earning power was at the peak, he had lived well, but he had also been careful to invest some of his money in enterprises that were certain to make him rich. For example, he bought a large tract of land in Mexico, said to be rich in minerals. Perhaps it was, but Harry's title to it turned out to be worthless. Similarly, he had had poor advice about the common stocks which he bought. Moreover, Ocean Home was the sort of estate which soaked up money; in the twenties it was one of the show places of Carmel, and when the flowers were out, it required the services of five men working six days a week to keep up the grounds. The settlement which he gave Helen Cooke when they were divorced was generous; but what finally ruined him was his loyalty to his elder brother, Lester, who, Harry could never forget, had taken care of him after their father died. And so when Lester, who had given up a good law practice in an attempt to amass a fortune as a California prune rancher, got into difficulties, Harry tried to help him. Year after year the prune ranch failed to pay, and year after year Harry secured Lester's notes at the bank, finally mortgaging even Ocean Home in a vain attempt to save his brother's business.[27]

Harry had a generous nature. Don Marquis recalled that when he was introduced to Harry at the Players Club the two men played a game of pool after which Harry asked him why he wasted stuff in a newspaper column that should go into fiction. Marquis explained he could not afford to give up newspaper work since it would take him several months to get started as a fiction writer and he needed every week's salary. "Any time," said Harry, "you want to start, let me know. I'll always have a couple of. thousand at your disposal." Marquis, who regretted not having taken him up, said that Harry really meant it, though the two had known each other only an hour or so when he made the offer.[28]

Even when his health and earning power were gone, as long as Harry had money he gave a good deal of it away. In 1935 he bought a house for an indigent female cousin in New Jersey; and the following year he helped Rose O'Neill to the extent of about $2,000 when her affairs began to go badly.[29] After she and Harry were divorced, Rose invented the Kewpie doll, from which she is said to have made a million dollars, but she was even more careless with money than Harry. In the days of her prosperity she endowed a table at the Brevoort Hotel in Greenwich Village where anyone who called himself a writer or an artist could, if he needed it, get a free meal.[30] She also bought a large house in Saugatuck, near Westport, Connecticut, christened it Carabas Castle after the marquis in Puss in Boots, and filled it with a choice company of young people, most of whom would today qualify as full-fledged beatniks.[31] In return for food and shelter, these beautiful souls admired Rose's poetry and sculpturing. There were many parties in the great hall at which Rose, as the master-mistress, as she liked to be called, dressed in a flowing velvet robe, her yellow hair (in her youth her hair was brown) curled on her shoulders, delighted her guests by reading poems like "The Ballad of Reading Gaol," "The City of Dreadful Night," and "The Hound of Heaven." Selections from Shakespeare, Samuel Butler, James Joyce, the Iliad and the Odyssey were also in her repertoire.[32] No doubt these evenings were edifying and uplifting, and it's a pity the depression finally put an end to them. She wrote Harry in November 1936 that the place "after fourteen years of great charm" was being taken away from her— "the ten acres of royal trees, the river, the gulls, the great room."[33] Some time before the ax finally fell, Harry had as we have seen helped her to the extent of perhaps two thousand dollars, and again in 1937 just after Rose's mother had died of cancer, he sent money to her in Missouri. "You can never know what you have done for me with this gift (hard to give I bet) —given me a little leeway to pull myself together—to sit down and grieve a moment before girding up for work," she wrote.[34] Between these two child-like adults there was a great deal of affection and sympathy, but also the sad knowledge that much as they admired one another they could not for any length of time get on together.

A pleasant feature of Harry's last decade was his friendship with Zilpha Riley. His interest in her began with a fan letter she sent him in August 1929. Harry replied; she answered; and the correspondence continued until 1937 when his failing health curtailed most of his letter writing. Her first letter was reticent, giving no hint that she was a widow of thirty-eight whose husband had died of tuberculosis two years before, and that she, too, a victim of that disease, was then and had been for some years a patient in a sanatorium in southern California. She was not in the habit of writing fan letters, but having recently undergone surgery and feeling quite depressed, she had happened to read an installment of *Lone Tree* in the *Post* which had lifted her spirits so much that she decided to write the author. Her letter simply thanked him for the joy and encouragement he had given her over the years— ever since she had read *Bunker Bean* in 1913. Harry replied he was glad she had liked the stories, "getting values that I know are there but that not so many people do get."[35] His reply seemed to indicate he would not mind her writing him again, and so she sent a second letter asking him what he thought about immortality. For a long time she had considered herself an infidel, but having seen so much suffering in the sanatorium, she now felt there was little point in living if the personality did not survive after death.

Harry was honest with her; he replied that he could see no evidence for a belief in personal immortality. He described in his first letter his own cure for the blues, which was "to glance up at an old brown skull that has long been on my desk, and then to picture beginnings—one of those remote spiral nebulae whirling through inconceivable time to throw off blobs that will become worlds and then say to the skull, 'You came out of *That*—you are what all the whirling is about.' And that gives me something to go on with, grasping those two extremes seems to answer so much."[36] Later he sent her Osborn's *Origin and Evolution of Life* and recommended that she read also the same author's *Men of the Old Stone Age*, which he called, "a good answer to all pessimists. . . . To me, and I've read it a lot, it's like a brace of cocktails."[37]

To Zilpha, a self-educated but intelligent woman, getting letters and books from Harry was, she said, "like going to college." He suggested that if she would write up her experiences in the sanatorium he would get them published. Tuberculosis fascinated him; it had touched many American families; his father and his eldest sister had died of it, and for a while in his youth he had feared it might be hereditary. Zilpha knew, however, that her chest condition had robbed her of the energy needed for writing, and so this scheme came to nothing. Still the correspondence continued. Harry discussed current literature with her. Biographies he seldom read, refusing to look at Ludwig's *Napoleon*. As for Van Wyck Brooks' *The Ordeal of Mark Twain*, he had never been able "to read two consecutive lines of Brooks about any one. He seems to be thinking about himself all the time he is writing and to have nothing important to say on that topic. To be sure he fools a lot of people by thinking and by writing muddily."[38] As for current fiction, he recommended all of Thornton Wilder except *The Woman of Andros*, which seemed to him "dry";[39] Julian Green, whose *Dark Journey* had just won a Harper's Ten Thousand Dollar Prize, he set down as "a young man who has made up his mind to be smarty and attract attention."[40] If he is "worth reading, then I'm a plumber."[41] There was much in the *Saturday Evening Post*, he told her, he could not read. An article by Will Rogers, "I passed up entirely after skimming the first half-column and finding not one sentence that took hold. Bill was using too many words and couldn't carry them off by an occasional and calculated lapse in grammar."[42] The best writing in the magazine "for a long time," he told her in the same letter, "was the opening story two weeks ago, 'Footlights—' something or other by Ben Hecht. A good story in itself, but what caught me was the writing of it. Hardly a sentence in it that wasn't electric. What a lot of boiling down and working over it required. I don't like Hecht's stuff usually . . . but this is perfect and unusual writing for the Post or any other magazine."[43] In his view "the biggest fiction writer now on the boards" was Tom Wolfe,[44] whose "Portrait of Bascom Hawke" in the April *Scribner's* "has some wonderful writing, though, as a whole unsymmetrical. Toward the end, too much 'I' and too much of New England, neither of value to the Portrait. I suspect he meant to use Bascom in a novel, then found he didn't fit, but the words that gave him out came, you may be sure, from nothing but a bloody sweat."[45]

When Zilpha, who had just read *Anna Karenina*, asked for Harry's opinion of Tolstoy, he advised her to "accept him as an artist, but remember that he didn't begin to preach about domestic relations until the years had put him where he could regard them only in an academic light. That is when all the moralizing is done; before senility the thing is taken as naturally as breathing by the strictest of them. So remember that, the next old fraud you encounter."[46]

Harry's favorite contemporary humorist was Kin Hubbard, whose Abe Martin cartoons Harry's sister May Miller often clipped and sent to him. These he passed along to Zilpha.[47]

Of humorous books Harry recommended James Stephens' *Crock of Gold* as "almost my favorite volume . . . no one ever wrote better prose and few ever wrote as well."[48] He also advised her to get *Zuleika Dobson* and Max Beerbohm's *Essays.* He sent her copies of Thorne Smith's *Turnabout, Night Life of the Gods,* and *Stray Lamb. Turnabout,* he told her, is "bawdy as hell, but still clean, if you know what I mean."[49]

The letters report that in May 1933, Smith, his wife, and two small girls, nine or so, visited at Ocean Home on their way back East from Hollywood where Smith had accumulated a great thirst for alcoholic beverages. "I had plenty of those, not having tasted anything of the sort for a year now, and again I have been made to recognize what a damper one sober man can be to a party of drinkers. They never recognize that his sympathies may be ardent, that he is probably crudely envious, but persist in imputing to him a severely critical attitude, even harshly condemnatory, resulting in repetitious apologies and protestations of admiration."[50] Still Harry thought Smith "a delightful chap, full of the stuff of his books."[51]

In May 1936 Zilpha was discharged from the sanatorium as an arrested case. Her victory over the disease was due, of course, to excellent nursing and medical care, but she believes that Harry's letters, beginning midway in her long battle at a time when she was feeling especially discouraged, helped to turn the tide. Certainly they did much for her morale.

Like most humorists, Harry was a complex, ambivalent person. One might call him a misanthropic sentimentalist. Behind a brusque manner he hid a soft heart. Early in life he seems to have built a protective wall around himself, past which he admitted only a few people—Tarkington, Sam Blythe, and perhaps Zilpha Riley. His own children felt that he never let them beyond his outer defenses until near the end of his life, after they had proved past all doubting that they could be trusted. Then they saw what a hopeful, kindly, but also extremely skeptical and lonely, man their father was.

Notes

CHAPTER SEVEN

A Writing Man

1. Letter from HLW to Rose O'Neill quoted in Rose's unpublished autobiography.

2. "The Fatal Ending," *Saturday Review of Literature*, II (November 14, 1925), 289.

3. *Ma Pettengill* (Garden City, New York: Doubleday, Page and Company, 1919), p. 168.

4. *New York Times*, March 31, p. 18, col. 2.

5. Letter, Tarkington to Ade, October 10, 1922. Ade papers. Purdue University.

6. CXCIX (May 14, 1927), 48–50.

7. "I Wish I'd Met," *Good Housekeeping*, CXIV (January, 1942), 39.

8. (New York: Cosmopolitan Book Corporation, 1924), p. 325.

9. *Ibid.*, p. 299.

10. *New York Herald Tribune Books*, September 29, 1929, p. 37; *New York Times*, September 15, 1929, p. 8.

11. Seattle, Washington, November 12, 1929. WP.

12. Letter, Stevens to the author, February 5, 1959.

13. "Your man Thomas Beer is the best thing that has come to the *Post* since the first wild cat." Letter, HLW to Lorimer, October 12, 1922, HSP. On February 5, 1934, George Milburn wrote HLW thanking him for a compliment Mencken said Wilson had made on one of Milburn's stories in the *American Mercury*. Milburn went on to say that as a boy he had read Wilson's stories with enthusiasm and that he owed a good deal to them. WP.

14. Letter, HLW to Stevens, August 15, 1929.

15. Letter, HLW to Zilpha Riley, January 13, 1930. WP.

16. Information from Leon Wilson. Lorimer paid $40,000 for *Cousin Jane* and $55,000 for *Lone Tree*.

17. Carbon copy of letter to H. L. Mencken, April 17, 1937. WP.

18. June 4, 1933. Original in TP.

19. "H. L.: A Writing Man," *Saturday Review of Literature,* XX (August 12, 1939), 10–11.

20. Harry nowhere specifically applies this phrase to the fictional characters of O'Neill or Anderson, but he does use it in a letter to Homer Croy congratulating him on *West of the Water Tower* which Harry said "is the hardest kind of novel to write; the novel of strictly character values. No help from conventional devices, no help from exotic or decadent personalities . . . merely a clash of plain people . . ." (March 14, 1923. Letter owned by Homer Croy.) We may infer that the writers who portrayed "exotic or decadent personalities" were O'Neill and Anderson.

21. HLW to Tarkington, San Francisco, n.d. 1934. TP. (Same letter as that referred to in note 32 Chapter One.)

22. *Carmel Pine Cone,* "An Artist with Words," August 31, 1939.

23. *Loc. cit.*

24. Letter, HLW to Julian Street, April 4, 1936. Street papers.

25. Information from Leon Wilson.

26. Letter, HLW to Julian Street, April 4, 1936. Street papers.

27. Letter, HLW to Tarkington, December 21, 1937. TP.

28. Edward Anthony, *O Rare Don Marquis, A Biography* (Garden City, New York: Doubleday & Company, Inc., 1962), pp. 356–357.

29. Letter, Rose O'Neill to Leon and Charis Wilson, April 13, 1938. WP.

30. Van Wyck Brooks, *Days of the Phoenix, the Nineteen Twenties I Remember* (New York: E. P. Dutton & Company, Inc., 1957), pp. 111–112.

31. Alexander King, "Kewpie Doll," *The New Yorker,* X (November 24, 1934), 22–26.

32. Alexander King, *May This House Be Safe from Tigers* (New York: Simon and Schuster, 1960), pp. 169–170.

33. Letter, Rose O'Neill to HLW, November 11, 1936. WP.

34. Letter, Rose O'Neill to HLW, undated, informing him of the death of her mother on March 15th. WP.

35. Author's interview with Zilpha Riley, March 29, 1958.

36. Letter, HLW to Zilpha Riley, September 16, 1929. WP. After HLW's death Mrs. Riley gave his letters to her to Charis and Leon.

37. September 29, 1931; October 30, 1931.

38. January 4, 1933.

39. March 29, 1932.

40. March 23, 1932.

41. March 29, 1932.

42. March 5, 1932.

43. *Loc. cit.*

44. March 29, 1932.

45. *Loc. cit.*

46. October 17, 1934.

47. September 29, 1931.

48. November 14, 1931.

49. December 18, 1931.

50. May 18, 1933.

51. *Loc. cit.*

The Old Man and the Sea

TOWARD THE END OF 1936 Harry began to suffer a series of little strokes. He had frequent dizzy spells and his memory was less and less dependable, but he did not forget that he had one more novel to write, a book which should sum up his conclusions about life. On January 3, 1937, he outlined his plan to Tarkington: "With my lame imagination I have never been able to picture our little earth as the only globe infested with life. . . . So, lately, it has seemed to me that the next big story to break will be interplanetary communication. With what we know of radio activity it is fairly certain that messages from other inhabited worlds are constantly pulsing through and around us. . . . So, someone soon, perhaps a kitchen lout, will hold up a dishpan at the nice angle, whereupon. . . ."[1] Harry felt that he could deliver "a real kick from this exposure of how an older world might regard us, if they ever found us worth a glance."[2] Realizing that he would need help with the scientific details, he appealed to Professor Clifford Cook Furnas, then of Yale's Sheffield Scientific School, and later Chancellor of the University of Buffalo, whose book, *The Next Hundred Years*, which he was using as a source, he had found

"continuously exciting."[3] He greatly admired Furnas's ability to
make abstruse ideas clear. "Not once did I have to read over a
sentence to learn what you were trying to tell me," he told the
scientist. "Often to be sure I would read over a paragraph or
a page just for the ride. But you have no Style—you just tell
it! Old John Ruskin would have pronounced your prose 'effec-
tive, perhaps, in a way barren.' Fifty years I've been trying to
write like that and still am."

What he asked of Professor Furnas was a scientifically described location for "the articulate planet," something that
could be put in a few words, and a plausible way of transport-
ing his commentator from outer space to the earth.

Professor Furnas, who had read *Professor How Could You!*
with keen delight, suggested that Harry have the stranger
come from one of the satellites of Sirius, only nine light years
away and that he be pushed to earth by the radiation pressure
of light after first reducing himself to a few molecules of his
germ cells. On earth he would quickly build himself a new
body while retaining his memories of his old life.[4] Harry liked
these ideas and on January 14th wrote thanking him for his
help and mentioning that among other things he was going
to have his say about capitalism and religion in the new book.

As he made plans for the novel, Harry grew apprehensive
that the *Post* might not want it for a serial, since Wesley Win-
ans Stout had replaced Lorimer as editor as of January 1, 1936.
In answer to one of his letters, Stout reassured him that the
magazine would always be interested in anything he wrote,[5]
and so Harry, like Hemingway's old man of the sea, settled
down to bring in the big one.

Harry read every day, taking notes for his book, but a year
later he had made no progress on the actual writing. Still his
zest for life continued strong. In the spring of 1937 H. L.
Mencken wrote that he might come west, and Harry replied,
urging him to stop at Ocean Home. "To whet your professed
interest in Carmel," he said, "I enclose some high-lights from

the last *Pine Cone*. But what might have been its feature story didn't get a word. For two weeks the town had its first official House. Two girls from outside launched the enterprise, though warned by old inhabitants they would be ruined by amateur competition from local oldish virgins—approximately. But the police have expelled them. And me planning to have the girls down for tea on a dullish Monday after they had begun to comprehend their milieu, aiming to win their confidence and get their reactions to the town and its profligates. They would have had a lot to tell and I am cheated of local color certain to have been high. . . ."[6] Mencken's trip, for some reason, did not materialize.

In the fall (of 1937) Witter Bynner, who had known Harry for many years, called at Ocean Home. "When I looked through the window and saw him playing solitaire, I had a misgiving which, however, evaporated as soon as the old grave smile met me in the doorway," Bynner wrote Rose O'Neill. "He told us about his life, and life it seems to be, although he sees no one but some people who sup with him every Sunday evening. Otherwise he lives his lone, [*sic*] dodging too much blood pressure and working away at a new novel. The best part of the visit was the genuine tone with which he told me that even on these terms he liked life better than ever, and that his only grievance against it was the fact that the time was approaching when he must give it up. I had seen other men, not so old as he bemoaning the debilities of age and isolation. Not he. There he stood at the prow of that house overlooking the sea, with his hand on the helm, a hearty skipper. Do tell him some time when you write him how good an experience it was for me."[7]

Harry's memory grew worse and worse. Though he continued to gather material for his story, he could do no actual writing on it. By April his vision was affected and he feared he was losing his mind. In this crisis the loyalty of his son and daughter meant everything to him. Like many other young people they were struggling in the depression—Charis and her husband, Edward Weston, the photographer, were living on a Guggenheim fellowship, and Leon had a minor editorial job with the movies—but they came home to do what they could to make H.L., as they called their father, comfortable and to try to straighten out the almost hopeless tangle of his affairs.

Under their care he got much better both physically and mentally. His vision came back to normal and his memory improved enough for him hopefully once more to set down notes for his novel, though every one except Harry now knew it would never be written. In January 1939 because the bank was about to take over Ocean Home, Charis moved her father into Carmel where he boarded with a practical nurse and her husband. There he had a large L-shaped room on the second floor overlooking the beach, fitted out with such familiar furnishings as his old bed, his card table, and his typing table.[8] Reading incessantly, he made notes for his book every day. Often, as he used to do at Ocean Home, he would pause in his work to gaze out at the tossing waves of the Pacific. Harry knew that his time was nearly up, but as he approached what he called "the ultimate take-off" he expressed no regrets and said that the only emotion he felt was "annoyance that I shall be expelled from a show that daily grows in interest."[9]

For exercise he took long walks. In June he felt strong enough to plan a camping trip with his landlord into California's Big Sur country. They expected to leave on the morning of the twenty-ninth, and the preceding evening Harry went to bed in cheerful mood. When called for breakfast he did not come. During the night he had had a severe brain hemorrhage and died quietly in his sleep.[10]

Harry had always regarded funerals as barbarous, and several years before, when his health first began to fail, he had stipulated that he be cremated and buried without ceremony. His children did as he wished. Sometime before his death Charis and her husband had been able to buy back from the bank a couple of acres of Ocean Home which lay across a ravine from the old house. There, on a spot within sight of the restless waves, Harry's ashes were buried.

Harry Leon Wilson was generous and brave. He worked hard, and earned a good deal of money, most of which he gave away. When in his later years poverty and ill health assailed him, he never lost the hope that he could still write a novel that would free him from his financial troubles. He took notes for that novel on the day he died. Booth Tarkington, the friend who knew him best, summed up his entire career in a phrase: "H.L. was," said Tarkington, "a writing man."

In an obituary editorial the *New York Times* said Harry "filled the country with laughter."[11] A writer who could do that deserves honor, but Harry never achieved fame. His great popularity, of course, cost him the esteem of the critics most of whom firmly believing that books which large numbers of the public love can't be good, ignored his work. To be sure there were exceptions. Here and there a perceptive reviewer like Malcolm Cowley[12] or William Lyon Phelps[13] pointed out that some of Wilson's fiction was better than the average product of the magazines, but no one scrutinized his work carefully. This reluctance to do so is understandable in view of his conspicuous limitations. Like most western humorists he is much too diffuse, spinning out anecdotes to the three or four thousand words demanded of stories in the *Post*. A more serious shortcoming is that the range of his interests is narrow. He made no comment on the League of Nations, the oil scandals of the Harding administration, the activities of the Ku Klux Klan, or the problems of minority groups—all topics which should have interested a man of Harry's talent. And yet in spite of their limitations, his books are worthy of attention, since they tell us a good deal about what the common man thought and how he felt in the nineteen-twenties.

Commentators on the period often seem to be laboring under the impression that there was a wide gap between the

attitudes and opinions of the common man and those who
thought of themselves as intellectuals. Actually, the gap existed mainly in the imagination of the so-called "civilized minority." One of the distinguishing marks of the saving rem-
nant, so Frederick Lewis Allen tells us, was disdain for the
movies.[14] Certainly, the thousands of readers who chuckled
over *Merton of the Movies* shared something of that disdain.
Or consider the common man's attitude toward success. Mencken's proclamation that success is largely a matter of luck
rather than of hard work and salubrious habits[15] could not
have come as a revelation of neglected truth to the devotees
of Ma Pettengill or old Ben Carcross. Many of Harry's readers
must have agreed with old Ben that "There ain't any big oil
men. There is only men that big oil happened to. Bill Hepburn
was a big brakeman on a fast freight. He got into a poker game
on one of his lay-overs and won sixty dollars. He took the
loser's cow in payment and then had to get a pasture for the
cow. They struck oil in the pasture. That's how Bill got to be
a big oil man. Anyone can if it happens."[16]

As for the common man's attitude toward the changing status of women, Ma Pettengill's ability to manage a ranch, smoke
cigarettes, and drink whiskey without losing the respect of the
community shows that he was not so "puritanical" as he has
been painted. Furthermore, the common man did not agree
with the alarmists who predicted that the new freedom would
destroy the home; in *Professor How Could You!* he saw the
joke in Mrs. Gale's remark that "The home is truly in danger
... I read it in the papers. Society is rotten to the core; the pop-
ping of champagne corks is heard on every hand. We are
dancing down the hill to destruction—there was a wonderful
drawing of the scene in the paper of last Sabbath—and according to the article that went with it I shall be surprised if the
home endures another hundred years. We live in a terrible
time." (p. 186)

Again consider religion. From reading Mencken, one might

well decide that the average provincial middle class American was a Bible-thumping fundamentalist. Yet in *Lone Tree* Ben Carcross's attitude toward immortality is as enlightened as Mencken's own: "If I had to go right now," Mr. Carcross tells his nurse, "I wouldn't be expecting the worst of it, but I don't throw in with a lot of people that have it all cut and dried. You take a notice in my paper there—resolutions of sympathy about the death of Aunt Selma Davis, put in by her lodge, one of those Daughters of something—kind of hen Masons they are. Starts off: 'It having pleased Almighty God to remove from our midst our dearly beloved sister' and so forth. You know I don't hold with that. Aunt Selma was the nicest old thing, always sitting up with folks, sickness or babies or anything. That old dame never had a thought about herself, and nobody can tell me Almighty God could have got any fun out of removing her. At least, if He did, He was hard up for a good time. But what is Aunt Selma getting out of it? That's what puzzles me. Do you reckon she was snuffed out like an animal?" (p. 61) Wilson goes on to give what comfort he can to his readers with the thought that as long as friends remember us we have a sort of immortality in their minds.

Aside from being an index to what the common man really thought about such important issues as success, divorce, and religion, Harry's stories are interesting as examples of the best popular art of the period. Highbrows often complain of the separation of the artist from his public in our society. In popular art there is no such alienation; Harry's audience, as his large fan mail shows, responded to him warmly. "Why in the hell don't you get to work?" wrote a stranger from Dallas, Texas after Harry's automobile accident had made writing difficult. "Do you realize, do you figure, do you know that— except for a movie Ma Pettengill and Ruggles and Cousin Egbert have, to all intents and purpose, died the death and vanished these dozen years? Do you know that hundreds . . . of people in Dallas and Fresno and Tampa . . . experienced an actual, tangible want—just as their tummies would lack, say salt—because you stubbornly and mulishly refuse and neglect to carry on with the three bulliest characters in American (or any other damn nation) literature?"[17]

Another reason for prizing Harry's work is for its firm command of the vernacular. His ear was as keen as Ring Lardner's; Ma Pettengill talks just as an old rancher should. A fascinating feature of his style is the colloquial flavor he imparts to it through the use of proverbs like "plow a straight furrow without stopping to pull weeds"; "a bird can't fly with one wing"; "tighter than Dick's hatband"; "there's more than one way to skin a cat"; "like a bat out of hell"; "put a bet down on every card from soda to hock"; "one crop of wild oats may be good for the ground, but two won't help it." Occasionally, he gives these old saws new teeth as in "a thrill a day keeps the doctor away," and sometimes he will manufacture a new one such as "I told him kind hearts were more than cornets or even saxophones."[18]

All of Harry's stories are good fun, suitable for family reading. Mrs. Penniman's impatient remark that her daughter's beau had been going with Winona for eight years but that "he'd never gone far with her,"[19] or Sooner Jackson's passing reference to selling a "side line consisting of the Hercules Little-Giant Vitalizer or Hindu Wizard Pill, warranted to renew the tired business man after his spring plowing"[20] is as close as he comes to the humor of sex. No doubt this reticence is one of the reasons Professor Howard Mumford Jones classified Harry as a "genteel humorist,"[21] and yet the label is a little misleading, for Harry liked to ridicule attempts to plant in the West, what Santayana called "the genteel tradition"—that is, the desiccated culture of New England and Europe. Thus he gets a good many laughs out of Mrs. Floud's insisting Cousin Egbert take notes on his impressions of Europe so that when he gets home he can read a paper before the Onwards and Upwards Club.

Harry's work is good popular art. It reflects the hope, the courage, and the innocence with which the American of his time viewed the world. Genial, cheerful humor of this sort seems to belong to an earlier, more youthful stage of society; at any rate, little of it is now produced in America. Other modes of the comic have long since replaced it, and Harry has had no successor. Ring Lardner, who when he began to write studied Harry's stories carefully,[22] developed into a bitter satirist. The disillusioned wits who built Ross's *New Yorker* were definitely hostile to anything which smacked of the soil; their work was largely written from a cosmopolitan, urban point of view.

Unlike the *New Yorker* but like the old *Puck*, the magazine on which Harry learned his trade, Harry tried to entertain not only the old lady from Dubuque but also her son and his family in Eureka, California and her son-in-law and daughter in Youngstown, Ohio. The America he charmed, an America of front porches, medicine shows, circuses, band concerts, trolley cars, barber shop quartets, and silent movies, has disappeared, taking our parents and grandparents with it. A country in which people could get excited about driving "a little old last year's car" must have been a pretty young and naive place, and on the whole perhaps it's just as well that it has matured into our fine new homogenized, suburbanized, welfare state. The economic ideas of Harry and his public were far behind the times. Yet if we want to know what those kindly good-natured people laughed at when of a Sunday afternoon they sat down on their front porches to relax over a magazine which was generally acknowledged to be "the national weekly," we can find out by turning to the stories of Harry Leon Wilson. Reading him is like leafing through the family album. His humor is as representative of its era as was the Model-T and as indigenous, the work of an artist whom the *Ogle County Reporter*[23] remembered as "one of the brightest boys in town."

From time to time throughout his career Harry Leon Wilson wistfully dreamed of writing a novel that would place his name

on the roll of the illustrious in literature, but whenever he began this masterpiece, it soon turned into something comical,
and, like his hero, Merton Gill, he had to reconcile himself to
being what God meant him to be—a comedian. As such he
made the most of his talent, zestfully but sympathetically
pointing up the incongruities between the common man's abilities and his aspirations, between his ideal of equality and his
wish to climb the status ladder, between his longing for security and his hankering for adventure. The stories that Harry
wrote on these themes will stand comparison with the best
examples of American humor. Comedies like *Ruggles of Red
Gap* and *Professor How Could You!* are not great literature,
but they are good fun and we would be poorer without them.

Notes

CHAPTER EIGHT

The Old Man and the Sea

1. Letter, HLW to Tarkington, January 3, 1937. TP.

2. *Loc. cit.*

3. Letter, HLW to C. C. Furnas, January 14, 1937. Owned by Chancellor
Furnas.

4. Letter, C. C. Furnas to HLW, January 5, 1937. WP.

5. Letter, HLW to C. C. Furnas, January 14, 1937. Owned by Chancellor
Furnas.

6. Carbon copy of letter, HLW to Mencken. April, 1937. WP.

7. Letter, Witter Bynner to Rose O'Neill, November 2, 1937. Quoted by
permission of Witter Bynner. Rose quoted the passage from Bynner in a
letter to HLW dated January 12, 1938. WP.

8. Letter, Charis Wilson to Booth Tarkington. February 3, 1939. TP.

9. Letter to Mencken cited in note 6 above.

10. *New York Times,* June 30, 1939, p. 18.

11. Obituary editorial, *New York Times,* June 30, 1939.

12. "A Lamb Among Wolves," *Saturday Review of Literature,* I (November 15, 1924), 280.

13. "As I Like It," *Scribner's,* LXXXVII (January, 1930), 104.

14. *Only Yesterday* (New York: Harper and Brothers, 1931), p. 228.

15. Oscar Cargill, *Intellectual America, Ideas on the March* (New York: The Macmillan Company, 1948), p. 493.

16. *Lone Tree,* p. 282.

17. Letter, L-- S— to HLW, Dallas, Texas, September 14, 1936. WP.

18. *Ma Pettengill,* pp. 92, 179; *Lone Tree,* p. 267; *Ruggles of Red Gap,* pp. 28, 59, 180, 250; *Oh Doctor!,* p. 48; *Professor How Could You!,* pp. 48, 138.

19. *The Wrong Twin,* p. 173.

20. *Professor How Could You!,* p. 254.

21. *Guide to American Literature and its Backgrounds Since 1890.* Second edition (Cambridge: Harvard University Press, 1959), p. 86.

22. Elder, p. 138.

23. February 10, 1892.

Bibliography

BOOKS BY HARRY LEON WILSON

Zigzag Tales from the East to the West. New York: Keppler and Schwarzmann, 1894.

The Spenders: A Tale of the third Generation. Boston: Lothrop Publishing Co., 1902.

The Lions of the Lord, a Tale of the Old West. Boston: Lothrop Publishing Co., 1903.

The Seeker. New York: Doubleday, Page and Company, 1904.

The Boss of Little Arcady. Boston: Lothrop, Lee & Shepard Co., 1905.

Ewing's Lady. New York: D. Appleton and Company, 1907.

The Man from Home, by Booth Tarkington and Harry Leon Wilson; with illustrations from scenes in the play. New York and London: Harper and Brothers, 1908.

Bunker Bean. Garden City, N. Y.: Doubleday, Page & Company, 1913.

Ruggles of Red Gap. Garden City, N. Y.: Doubleday, Page & Company, 1915.

The Man from Home; a novel by Harry Leon Wilson founded on the play by N. Booth Tarkington and Harry Leon Wilson. New York: D. Appleton and Company, 1915.

Somewhere in Red Gap. Garden City, N. Y.: Doubleday, Page & Company, 1916.

Ma Pettengill. Garden City, N. Y.: Doubleday, Page & Company, 1919.

Life. The seventeenth grove play of the Bohemian Club of San Francisco, as performed by its members in the Bohemian Grove, Sonoma County, California, on the twenty-eighth night of June, nineteen hundred and nineteen. San Francisco: The Bohemian Club, 1919.

The Gibson Upright. Garden City, New York: Doubleday, Page & Company, 1919.

The Wrong Twin. Garden City, New York and Toronto: Doubleday, Page & Company, 1921.

Merton of the Movies. Garden City, New York: Doubleday, Page & Company, 1922.

So This is Golf! New York: Cosmopolitan Book Corporation, 1923.

Oh, Doctor! New York: Cosmopolitan Book Corporation, 1923.

Ma Pettengill Talks. Garden City, New York: Garden City Publishing Company, 1923.

Professor How Could You! New York: Cosmopolitan Book Corporation, 1924.

Tweedles, a comedy by Booth Tarkington and Harry Leon Wilson. New York: S. French; London: S. French, ltd., 1924.

Cousin Jane. New York: Cosmopolitan Book Corporation, 1925.

Lone Tree. New York: Cosmopolitan Book Corporation, 1929.

How's Your Health? a comedy in three acts by N. Booth Tarkington and Harry Leon Wilson. New York, New York, Los Angeles, California: S. French, inc.; London: S. French, ltd., 1930.

Two Black Sheep. New York: Cosmopolitan Book Corporation, 1931.

When in the Course—. New York: H. C. Kinsey & Company, Inc., 1940.

Index